A GIRL CALLED VINCENT

A Girl Called Vincent

The Life of Poet
Edna St. Vincent Millay

KRYSTYNA PORAY GODDU

Copyright © 2016 by Krystyna Poray Goddu
All rights reserved
Published by Chicago Review Press Incorporated
814 North Franklin Street
Chicago, Illinois 60610

ISBN 978-1-61373-172-7

Library of Congress Cataloging-in-Publication Data

Goddu, Krystyna Poray.
  A girl called Vincent : the life of poet Edna St. Vincent Millay /
Krystyna Poray Goddu.
      pages cm
  Includes bibliographical references and index.
  ISBN 978-1-61373-172-7 (cloth)
  1. Millay, Edna St. Vincent, 1892–1950. 2. Poets, American—
20th century—Biography. 3. Women and literature—United
States—History—20th century. I. Title.
  PS3525.I495Z6365 2016
  811'.52—dc23
  [B]
                    2015032432

Interior design: Sarah Olson

Permission to reprint photographs and quoted text from poems,
letters, and diaries, published and unpublished, is granted by
The Permissions Company, Inc., on behalf of Holly Peppe, Literary Executor, The Millay Society. www.millay.org.

Printed in the United States of America
5 4 3 2 1

This book is dedicated to the memory of Jack Scaparro (1935–2012)
fellow writer, fierce champion, longtime friend

"In your day, this moment is the sun
Upon a hill, after the sun has set."

—Edna St. Vincent Millay

Contents

Introduction

When I was about 12 years old, I found these words in a poetry book:

All I could see from where I stood
Was three long mountains and a wood.
I turned and looked another way
And saw three islands in a bay.

The words were simple, and they made me want to be in that beautiful place where I could see three islands in a bay, three long mountains, and a wood. I kept reading. "Over these things I could not see / These were the things that bounded me."

Hmm. Now I wasn't sure what the poem was really about. It was a very long one—more than 200 lines—but the rhythm of the words, the very clear images, and the stirring emotions kept me reading. By the time I had finished it, I was puzzled, moved, and intrigued all at once. I started reading it again.

That poem was Edna St. Vincent Millay's "Renascence," and I have never forgotten the experience of reading it in my attic bedroom, over and over again, feeling chills and heat and fascination. I was a young girl who believed herself a poet, and this poem was deeply inspiring.

I started to learn more about Edna St. Vincent Millay, and found out that she was only 19 years old when she wrote this poem. Her life seemed amazing to me. It sounded romantic and exciting. Known to her family and friends as Vincent, she was a tiny, red-haired, high-spirited girl who loved to write poems, plays, and music, and to perform. She grew up to be a tiny, red-haired, high-spirited woman, who became known as one of America's greatest poets. When she appeared onstage to recite her poetry, audiences went wild at the sight of the slight figure in the long silk gown. Men and women sent her flowers and love notes. Can you imagine an audience going wild for a poet? That was how people reacted to Vincent.

How did that little girl become such a sensation, who bewitched audiences with her words, her voice, and her appearance? How did a girl raised in poverty in rural Maine grow into an international celebrity? And how did she come to write poems that still make us tingle when we read them today?

There is one word that captures the essence of Edna St. Vincent Millay and her writing: *passion*. She was a girl who, from her earliest years, threw herself at the world, taking everything she wanted from it and turning her life and all its experiences into stirring poems. One of her most well-known poems sums up her approach to life:

> *My candle burns at both ends;*
> *It will not last the night;*
> *But ah, my foes, and oh, my friends—*
> *It gives a lovely light!*

The life of Edna St. Vincent Millay was filled with adventure, art, beauty, love, and, sometimes, pain. I believe that her story teaches us to face life with eagerness and honesty, to work for what we desire, to be brave in small moments and big ones, to live as we believe is right for us, and to appreciate and exhilarate in the world's beauty.

When Vincent was 20, in a letter to a new friend who questioned whether her poem was about something she found in a book, she wrote indignantly, "I'll slap your face! I see things with my own eyes, just as if they were the first eyes that ever saw, and then I set about to tell, as best I can, just what I've seen."

In this book, I try to look at Vincent's story with my own eyes—both the eyes of the girl who discovered her poetry and those of the woman who appreciates what it took to live her life—and to tell her story as best I can.

A Girl Called Vincent

1892–1904

As the baby emerged, she appeared to be wearing a thin, translucent veil over her face. The doctor attending the birth quickly reached out his hand to wipe away the transparent covering, and the newborn gave her first lusty cry.

Her family instantly grasped the omen: this was no ordinary child who had come into the world. The red-haired infant had been born with a caul, a thin membrane covering her face, a rarity and a sign—for those who believe in such things—that the person is destined for an extraordinary life.

For Edna St. Vincent Millay, the omen proved true. Born to Cora Buzzell Millay and Henry Tollman Millay a few minutes after six o'clock on the morning of

February 22, 1892, in the small coastal city of Rockland, Maine, Vincent, as she quickly came to be called, did lead an extraordinary life. Passionate, rebellious, and hungry for experience of every kind, she became renowned

A baby photo of Edna St. Vincent Millay. Her mother chose the name Vincent to honor St. Vincent's Hospital in New York City. *Edna St. Vincent Millay Papers, Manuscript Division, Library of Congress, Washington, DC*

throughout the world as much for her zealous spirit as for her fervent poetry.

Cora's younger sister Clem, who had witnessed Vincent's birth, wrote to their beloved brother Charlie to announce the news and to share the baby's name. Cora had chosen "Vincent" in gratitude to St. Vincent's Hospital in New York City, where Charlie had been nursed back to health after a traumatic physical ordeal just days before the baby's birth.

Not long after Vincent's arrival, Cora, Henry, and Clem moved inland to Henry's hometown, the village of Union, where his parents still lived. They invited Charlie, who remained weak, to stay with them until he was completely well. That summer Charlie came to live with the young family. Surrounded by loving comfort, Vincent rested in a low hammock in the yard as the adults sang away the warm days, filling the baby's ears with melodic tunes and harmonious ballads. Sometimes her babbling tones joined in.

Some of the first sounds Vincent heard that summer, mixed with the voices making music, would have been those of the natural world resonating around her, sounds she later put into her poems: "the rising of the wind / In the trees before the rain," "the woodcock's watery call," "the grey wood-pecker taps and bores," "noisy and swift the small brooks run."

She was the only child for just a short time, and couldn't remember life without her sisters. Vincent wasn't even two when Norma Lounella was born in

December 1893, and the youngest, Kathleen Kalloch, arrived in May 1896. The sisters looked very different from each other; dark-haired Kathleen was always called the prettiest, Norma was blonde and sang beautifully, while Vincent had hair the color of fire and a personality to match. From her earliest years, she was a girl of strong emotions—exuberant laughter and intense rage. There was never anything calm about Vincent; her sisters used to say that she had a bee chasing her. In her fury, she could be terrifying. Once Norma and Kathleen watched in horror as Vincent, overtaken by sudden anger, ran outside with a kitchen knife and thrust it into a tree trunk.

The sisters were each other's best friends, calling each other, for decades to come, by silly nicknames that came from one of their favorite childhood songs, an old college tune Cora liked to sing to them. "There was a man who had two sons, and those two sons were brothers. Josephus was the name of one and Bohunkus was the other." For the rest of their lives, Vincent was Sefe and Norma was Hunk. Kathleen became, mysteriously, Wump.

It's no surprise that all three sisters learned to sing, play the piano, perform, and write poetry when they were very young; these were Cora's passions, and she shared them with her daughters as naturally as she breathed. Cora's poems had appeared in New England publications, and before she married she had given concerts locally, advertising them as "Miss Buzzell's Concerts." In

Even as a young child, Vincent was a girl of strong emotions.
*Edna St. Vincent Millay Papers, Manuscript Division, Library of Congress,
Washington, DC*

fact, she had met handsome Henry—blonde, blue-eyed,
and broad-shouldered—at a dance where she was one of
the musicians.

Cora continued to play and perform after becoming a
wife and mother, and it wasn't long before her daughters

Vincent's mother, Cora Buzzell Millay, is shown here a year before her marriage. *Edna St. Vincent Millay Papers, Manuscript Division, Library of Congress, Washington, DC*

started appearing with her. When she sang in a quartet at the town hall in Union one February evening, Vincent, a few weeks shy of her fifth birthday, performed a solo: "The little maid milking her Cow."

Another time, Vincent and Norma performed the cakewalk together, high-stepping, arms akimbo, to an oompah rhythm played by Cora. The cakewalk was a dance made popular through minstrel shows, and audiences applauded the talented little sisters strutting their stuff. "I'd bend down—all this in rhythm to the music Mother was playing on the piano, or the organ, maybe— one! two! I'd tie Vincent's shoe," Norma recalled. "Then we'd throw back our heads, take arms and strut and cakewalk down."

Vincent adored her mother and wanted to do everything she did. They didn't have a piano, but they did have an organ. Cora, always keen to nourish her daughters' talents, taught Vincent to play, even though her little legs were too short to reach the pedals. The two of them spent hours together at the instrument, Cora working the pedals while determined Vincent, eyes shining, learned to make the keys sing.

Before Vincent was five, Cora had taught the eager girl to read both music and poetry. Some of the first poetry she read by herself was from Shakespeare's *Romeo and Juliet*, and, difficult as the language was for a small child, its beauty made her hold her breath and its fervor hit her with physical force. "It knocked the wind clear out of me," Vincent remembered later. It was the first time she felt what would become an increasingly familiar urgency over the years—to use words to create that kind of power. One of the things she would write magnificently about throughout her life was nature, and her first poem was on that subject.

> *One bird on a tree,*
> *One bird come to me.*
> *One bird on the ground,*
> *One bird hopping round.*
> *One bird in his nest,*
> *One bird took a rest.*

Her poem may not have been very Shakespearean, but it certainly had the mark of somebody who had been reading poetry, had absorbed the concepts of rhyme and meter, and knew how to use them. For a girl not yet five, it was a great poem.

Vincent's father,
Henry Tollman Millay.
Edna St. Vincent Millay Papers,
Manuscript Division, Library of
Congress, Washington, DC

While Cora was playing music and reading poetry with her little girls, Henry was supposed to be supporting the household. He was good-looking, charming, and easygoing with a slow grin, and he could always make Cora laugh. Henry loved to fish and play poker, though, much more than he liked to work. For a while he had a good job as superintendent of schools in Union, but even when he had a job, he often gambled away his earnings. Money got tighter and tighter, until finally the awful, embarrassing day came when the Millays could no longer afford to live in their house. It was sold, and the family of five moved in with a neighbor across the street. To help pay the bills, Cora gave music lessons.

In the early years of their marriage, Cora and Henry had gaily danced and sung together, and he had taught her to play a mean game of cards, too. But with every day that passed, she understood more strongly that Henry was incapable of sharing the responsibilities of raising a family with her. She struggled to pay the bills, caring for their three daughters by herself, and didn't complain about him to anybody.

By 1900, Cora made the difficult decision that she and the girls would be better off without Henry. Just before Vincent's eighth birthday, Cora asked him to leave. In the early years of the 20th century, it was highly unusual for a married couple to divorce—and even more unusual for it to be the woman's decision. Cora's own mother had divorced her father when Cora was a teenager, however, and she and her siblings had been brought up by their mother alone. She knew exactly how hard being a single mother would be, but she also knew she could raise the girls better without Henry.

Vincent didn't talk, or write, about her parents' separation. It was not until she was 31, and had just won the Pulitzer Prize for poetry, that she referred to the day her father left. She slipped the memory into a rhapsody about nature in a letter to her friend Tess Root. "All my childhood is in those bayberry-bushes, & queen-of-the-meadow, or maybe you called it hardhack, & rosehips. And cranberries—I remember a swamp of them that made a short-cut to the railroad station when I was seven. It was down across that swamp my father went, when my mother told him to go & not come back. (Or maybe she said he might come back if he would do better—but who ever does better?)"

Henry agreed to leave the family without argument and promised to help financially, though Cora probably knew in her heart he would never keep that promise. He

moved to Kingman, about 140 miles north of Union—
a very long distance in those days. At eight years old,
being the daughter who could write best, Vincent took
on the responsibility of writing to him regularly, and he
replied, but not as regularly. In May 1900 he chastised
himself: "Your papa ought to be ashamed of himself for
not answering your nice letter soon, and I guess he is.
. . . How does Norma get along at school? I suppose she is
getting to be a pretty good scholar and Wump I suppose
is awful busy making mud pies. I want you to kiss them
both for papa and mamma, too. Tell Mamma that papa
. . . has got started to earning money at last."

But by July he still hadn't sent any money. Instead he
wrote Vincent: "Tell Mama . . . Papa is earning quite a
lot of money only he can't get it very fast yet."

His letters started sounding all alike. The one he sent
in November began, "It seems an awful long time to
Papa since he saw his little girls, but he could not help
it." All the letters were addressed to Vincent, and much
as he claimed he wanted to see his little girls, it would be
11 years before Vincent saw her father again.

Four Homes in Two Years

It was now solely up to Cora to support the family. Before she was married, she had earned money weaving hairpieces—a skill she had learned from her mother, who had run a hairdressing business. But now Cora decided to apply for nursing jobs; her sister Clem had been studying nursing in their hometown of Newburyport, Massachusetts, and had given Cora her notes to learn from.

In the autumn of 1900 Cora and the girls left Union and moved to Rockport, a coastal village about 12 miles east, where they rented the upper half of a house overlooking the harbor and where Cora believed nursing work would be more plentiful. Soon jobs did come her way, but often they were in other towns, like Rockland or

Camden, far enough away that she might have to spend the night—sometimes more than one—there. It tore at her heart to leave her daughters, but she didn't have much choice, and Cora felt lucky that she had neighbors to take care of them when she was gone. The nursing was grueling—she assisted with surgery and childbirth, took care of wounds, and cleaned up patients who suffered from nausea or diarrhea—and she usually earned one dollar a day. Still, it was money they wouldn't have had otherwise, and she had to do it.

The girls missed her terribly when she was away, and she missed them just as much. Cora asked them to write her cheerful notes, to make her work feel a little easier. On November 7, Vincent sent her a very chatty letter, focusing, naturally, on her achievements in music and writing (although not showing much evidence of her good grades in spelling). "Dear Mama: I thought I would write to you and tell you how I am I am getting along all right in school but in my spelling-blank I had 10 and 10 and then 9 and I felt auful bad because I thought I wuld have a star I am getting along all right and so is Norma and Kathleens cold is better now I went to practice and a boy called me a little chamipion and I asked him what he meant and he said because I was the best singer and I thanked him."

Vincent had a wicked sense of humor and was a great tease. Not even authority figures were spared her sly tongue. In the same letter to her mother, she recounted ribbing her teacher about once dating Cora's cousin. "When teacher and I were alone I said you have not called on mama yet and she said she is away and then she asked me how you knew her and of course I had to tell her and I said I guess you used to go around with George Keller [Cora's cousin] and she blused red as a June rose and then she asked me If I had ever rode in [h]is tire wagon an[d] I said I knew she had and she said oh yes. . . . Lots of love to you your loving daughter Vincent."

Amusing encounters like those were rare for the sisters in Rockport, though. Newcomers, they didn't have friends, and when Cora was away, they felt almost like orphans. As always, they took comfort in each other's company, singing together, drawing birds and wildflowers, making up plays and games. They would spend the rest of their young lives by the sea, but this was their first experience by the water, and they reveled in the salty air and the sound of the surf. As an adult, Vincent would miss the ocean acutely, lamenting in a poem she called "Exiled" that she was:

Wanting the sticky, salty sweetness
Of the strong wind and shattered spray;
Wanting the loud sound and the soft sound
Of the big surf that breaks all day.

In September 1901 Cora left for a difficult nursing case on the island of Vinalhaven, 15 miles across the bay from the mainland. Today it takes more than an hour to get to Vinalhaven by ferry, and in 1901 the island was much more remote. When the weather was rough, boats couldn't make the trip. For the girls—and Cora, too—it felt like she was very far away.

Cora had been on Vinalhaven for more than a month when the sisters, one by one, began to get stomachaches. Soon they were feeling feverish, too, but Cora always left firm instructions that they were not to whine or grumble while she was gone, so Vincent didn't dare to write her with their complaints. She wrote only that she didn't feel very well, and neither did Norma or Kathleen.

Cora was overworked, and her patience was thin. She didn't have the energy to worry about her daughters while tending to her patient, but she couldn't ignore Vincent's letter.

"You said you were almost sick," she wrote back, "and that made me anxious about you. I cannot write much now as I am very busy; but I want you to write me at once and tell me if you are well."

Cora must have soon suspected what might be ailing her girls, because she abruptly left Vinalhaven to journey back to Rockport, traveling by horse and carriage, then by boat—a long, slow trip in those days—and the final few, but anxious, miles on land again. By the time she arrived, she found all three of her daughters suffering from the early symptoms of typhoid fever: high temperatures, stomach pain, and diarrhea.

Cora was terrified. She had nursed enough patients with the disease to know that there was no real treatment for typhoid fever, only alcohol baths and cold cloths to try to keep the fever in control. She also knew firsthand that one out of every eight or ten people who contracted typhoid fever died of it.

Today only about 400 people a year get typhoid fever in the United States, but in 1901 there were two major outbreaks. Tens of thousands were stricken with the bacterial infection, which spreads through contaminated food, drink, or water. Today we know that typhoid fever cannot be spread by mere contact with a sick person,

The sisters pose with their schoolmates in Rockport. Vincent is at the top left, Norma is third from left in the top row, and Kathleen is second from the left in the middle row. *Edna St. Vincent Millay Papers, Manuscript Division, Library of Congress, Washington, DC*

but in 1901 many people believed it could, so Cora had to nurse her daughters alone. She never left their bedsides—she even slept sitting up by them. The illness took its usual frightening course; their fevers rose and their diarrhea became more severe as the days and weeks went on. They were so weak and tired they could barely lift their heads off their pillows. Their hair fell out.

While their illnesses wore on, Cora tried to keep the girls and everything around them extremely clean. A Contagious Disease Bulletin on Typhoid Fever issued by Johnson & Johnson that year instructed, "More than ordinary cleanliness must be observed if typhoid is to be gotten rid of. Surgical cleanliness . . . while perhaps impossible practically, must be the aim."

Vincent, Norma, and Kathleen lay in bed, fevers raging, for nearly a month. In spite of Cora's tenacious, tireless nursing, in mid-October even their doctor had no hope that any of them would survive. But suddenly, miraculously, their fevers broke and they began, slowly, to get better.

Strong and independent as Cora was, she couldn't face the idea of a winter alone in Rockport after the physically and emotionally exhausting experience of nursing her three daughters back to health. She took the girls 150 miles south to her brother Charlie's home on Ring Island, Massachusetts, just across the Merrimac River from Newburyport. Charlie was recently married, and Clem now lived in Newburyport, too, with their greataunt Susan Todd.

Enveloped and embraced by their mother's family, Vincent, Norma, and Kathleen started a new life—again. They went to school on Ring Island where, their hair just growing in again, they were stared at by the other children. Strangers to their schoolmates, lacking a true home of their own, and still weak from the typhoid, they had few playmates besides each other and drew together even more fiercely.

Now in the fourth grade, Vincent threw herself into writing new poems, and she was hungry for reading material. During that winter at Uncle Charlie's house, she spent the extravagant sum of two dollars to subscribe to *Harper's Young People* magazine, which originally described itself as "a weekly journal of amusement and instruction." She wrote a careful and mature note, including the date and her address (Ring's Island was considered part of Salisbury), and using a form of her name that she would use for most of her writing for many years to come, one that made it unclear whether she was a boy or a girl (but certainly created the assumption that the writer was a boy).

Salisbury, Mass.
Feb. 12, 1902
Harper & Brothers
322 Pearl St.
New York.

Gentlemen:—I wish to subscribe for "Harpers Young People" and here enclose $2.00 for *that purpose. I wish to begin with the next number and so have written as soon as I found your residence by reading one of your books.*

Respectfully yours.
E. Vincent Millay.

She didn't seem to know that *Harper's Young People*, which had been published as a weekly illustrated magazine since 1879, had ceased publication three years earlier. Hopefully she got her two dollars back.

Comforting as it was to live with Charlie and his wife, Jennie, by summer Cora felt emotionally—and financially—stronger and could afford to rent a house of her own. She found a shabby square farmhouse, built in the 1800s on the banks of the river. It was near Charlie and Jennie's home, and even though Cora and the girls only lived in it for a few months, Vincent relished the beauty of its surroundings—the backyard that led to the marshes and the front yard filled with flowers. Living there, she could indulge in her love of nature, mentally storing up the images that would fill her poetry, like these from a poem titled "Journey" in her 1921 collection, *Second April*.

Eager vines
Go up the rocks and wait; flushed apple-trees
Pause in their dance and break the ring for me;
Dim, shady wood-roads, redolent of fern
And bayberry, that through sweet bevies thread
Of round-faced roses, pink and petulant,

Look back and beckon ere they disappear.
Only my heart, my heart responds. . . .

But far, oh, far as passionate eye can reach,
And long, ah, long as rapturous eye can cling,
The world is mine: blue hill, still silver lake,
Broad field, bright flower, and the long white road;
A gateless garden, and an open path:
My feet to follow, and my heart to hold.

In the autumn they had to leave the romantic house on the river. This time they moved into town, taking up residence at 78 Limerock Street—it was their fourth home in two years. Their first winter there was the coldest in history. Temperatures fell to 40 degrees below zero, and there was a coal shortage. Sometimes Vincent had to steal over to the abandoned rundown house next door and tear off handfuls of shingles to keep the fire going in their tiny kitchen.

That winter it was Cora who got sick—with a severe case of influenza. The doctor told them it was due to overwork and undernourishment, and the cold temperatures didn't help. Aunt Clem came over regularly with food she had cooked, but with Cora bedridden, the daily responsibilities were Vincent's. Even though she was not yet 11, she had to take care of Norma and Kathleen, make sure all three of them got to school, keep the house clean and as warm as possible, and make sure everybody was fed when Aunt Clem didn't appear. Cora recalled in her diary that Vincent learned how to bake excellent yeast bread that winter.

Reluctantly, Vincent was learning how to run the household, albeit in her own fashion. She might have been looking back at her childhood housekeeping when, in her late 20s, she wrote the poem she called "Portrait by a Neighbor."

Before she has her floor swept
Or her dishes done,
Any day you'll find her
A-sunning in the sun!

It's long after midnight
Her key's in the lock,
And you never see her chimney smoke
Till past ten o'clock!

She digs in her garden
With a shovel and a spoon,
She weeds her lazy lettuce
By the light of the moon,

She walks up the walk
Like a woman in a dream,
She forgets she borrowed butter
And pays you back cream!

Her lawn looks like a meadow,
And if she mows the place
She leaves the clover standing
And the Queen Anne's lace!

Although Vincent could later write teasingly about her housekeeping efforts, that winter was another frightening season for the close-knit family. It was hard not to feel overwhelmed by distress when their usually strong, stoic mother was so frail and anxious. And being a nurse, Cora knew how sick she was. She wrote in her diary (referring to herself as "the mother"): "And many a night the mother went to bed when she did not have much idea of seeing the morning. But she did not tell them so."

As the cold weeks went by, though, and trees began to turn green again, Cora recovered—just in time to nurse Kathleen, who suddenly contracted a high fever and was once again proclaimed to be near death. She had been stricken by the disease that later came to be known as polio, but unlike many children who were afflicted by it, she survived and slowly grew healthy.

When Cora knew that Kathleen was out of danger, she went back to nursing, supplementing it with the hair work she still did from time to time. Her nursing jobs again kept her from home for days at a time, and by the time she was 12, Vincent was in charge when Cora was away. Playing "mother" was physically exhausting and emotionally draining, and sometimes more than Vincent could bear. Her only solace came from the moments she stole for music, poetry, and nature.

A Very Young Housekeeper

1904–1907

L ate in 1904 Cora moved her household of little women back to Maine, this time to Camden, a beautiful midcoastal town on Penobscot Bay. Once upon a time it had been a great center of shipbuilding, but by the time the Millay family took up residence there, only one shipyard remained. A popular summer resort and port for fishing boats as well as pleasure craft, the town sits at the base of the Camden Hills. The tallest of the three mountains that tower over the water is Mount Megunticook, but the best views are from the summit of rocky Mount Battie, from which you can see not only the town of Camden but all of Penobscot Bay, sprinkled with little islands.

Cora chose Camden because she had worked there over the summer, caring for John Tufts, a musical composer and pianist, and she knew the doctors would have nursing work for her in the area. What's more, her aunt Clara ran a boardinghouse on the outskirts of town for the mill laborers who worked at the six wool mills that were now Camden's primary employers. Even though Vincent was 12 years old and experienced at running the household, it would ease Cora's mind to know Aunt Clara was close by to watch out for the girls when she was away on nursing assignments.

The house they rented at 100 Washington Street was near Aunt Clara's, the mills, and the Megunticook River, in the poorest part of town known, fittingly, as Millville. Sometimes the wool mills spilled their dyes into the river, turning it vivid, unnatural colors. Vincent and her sisters liked to swim in the river, but only on days when the water ran clear. The house was tiny—two rooms upstairs and two rooms downstairs—and on such low, sloping ground that when the river overflowed, the kitchen floor flooded. Only the upstairs of the house was heated, so if the river overflowed in the winter, the kitchen floor would freeze over and Vincent, Norma, and Kathleen could enjoy their own private skating rink.

The brown frame house sat alone in a large field. There were shades but no curtains at the windows. The only plumbing was in the kitchen, which also had a cooking stove, although it didn't give out enough warmth to heat the downstairs. Next to the kitchen was the dining room, which was also the library and music room, filled as it was with Cora's book collection and a small upright piano. The living room upstairs—which housed the only real source of heat, a coal stove—doubled as Cora and Kathleen's bedroom, while Vincent and Norma shared the second upstairs room. As soon as the weather got cold, any food that could freeze and spoil had to be taken upstairs to the living room: milk, potatoes, onions, bread, butter. Moving the food back and forth was a daily chore during the cold months.

The outdoors, however, was a never-ending source of natural beauty. The girls loved playing hide-and-seek in the long grass of the meadows, picking blueberries in summer and apples in autumn, and skating on the thickly frozen ponds in winter. They hiked up the gentle slope of Mount Battie, taking the trail out of town that started not far from their house.

Each season had its glories. Spring brought black chokeberry with its dark berries and then the fiery-colored wild columbine. In the summer the purple cone-flowers arrived, followed by the lighter purple, pink, and rosy New England asters. The blazing red and gold leaves of autumn never failed to render Vincent breathless. Maine's native white birch, white pines, and red maple trees grew everywhere.

Vincent, Norma, and Kathleen enrolled in the Elm Street School, where tiny Vincent turned out to be one of the best students in the school. The first composition she wrote for her teacher, Miss Emma Harrington, was so good that the teacher suspected she must have had help with it. Not wanting to voice her suspicions, she asked the girl if her mother had seen this fine piece of writing. Vincent saw through the question immediately.

"Excuse me, Miss Harrington," she said, "but I can tell that you think I didn't write that composition. Well, I did! But the only way I can prove it will be to write the next one you assign right here, in front of you. And I promise that it will be as good as this one, and maybe better."

Vincent had already been submitting her work to *St. Nicholas* magazine, to which she and her sisters had subscribed the winter before. Since the magazine's founding in the 1870s, *St. Nicholas* had been exposing children to the work of some of the finest writers of the day, such as Mark Twain, Rudyard Kipling, Louisa May Alcott, and Jack London. The magazine's St. Nicholas League invited children to submit their own work for publication and prizes—gold and silver medals, as well as cash. Vincent was interested in both the prizes and the cash. And publication, of course.

Cora was getting lots of nursing work, though she was still only earning about $10 a week, and almost all the jobs took her out of town for days—sometimes even weeks—on end. She wrote to her daughters regularly, reminding them of their chores and encouraging them in their attitudes. She wanted them to be merry and enjoy life, even with its hardships. She suggested they make up a song to accompany the seemingly endless dishwashing, and Vincent came up with one, naming it

"Miss Lane"—short for *miscellaneous*. One sister washed, another dried, and the third did miscellaneous pots, pans, and milk bottles, all three singing:

> *I'm the Queen of the Dish-pan*
> *My subjects abound.*
> *I can knock them about*
> *And push them around,*
> *And they answer with naught*
> *But a clattering sound;*
> *I'm the Queen of the Dish-pan*
> *Hooray!*

The chorus followed.

> *For I've pots and pans*
> *And kettles galore.*
> *If I think I'm done*
> *There are always some more,*
> *For here's a dozen*
> *And there's a score.*
> *I'm the Queen of the Dish-pan,*
> *Hooray!*

It might seem like fun to live without an adult telling you what to do all the time, but for Vincent and her sisters it was a mixed delight. They could eat and sleep when they chose, and play games instead of doing their schoolwork if they felt like it, but all three of them ached for their mother. Often at night they slept in the same bed together, both for comfort and for warmth.

Every time Cora returned home, it was like a celebration—and part of the advance celebrating always involved cleaning the house. Vincent made up games for cleaning, too; one of them was called "Corner." When a room needed a thorough cleaning, each of the girls took a corner and began cleaning toward the middle of the room. When they met in the center, all three girls attacked the final corner together.

One winter, soon after her 13th birthday, Vincent went to meet Cora at the home of the composer and pianist John Tufts, the man Cora had been nursing back to health after his serious surgery the previous summer. Mr. Tufts had retired from teaching piano at the New England Conservatory and now lived in an elegant house on Chestnut Street, where he had, naturally, a fine piano.

While waiting for her mother, Vincent—whose love for piano playing had only intensified throughout her childhood—couldn't resist trying out the instrument. She sat down and played a composition of her own, with her usual passion. The pianist, recognizing an unusual mix of talent and fervor, offered to give Vincent piano lessons for free, in gratitude for the excellent care Cora had given him during his long recovery. Vincent was elated; her hands were small for piano playing, but she tried to make up for their size by working hard at her lessons and at practicing, hoping and praying that they would grow to stretch a full octave.

Clockwise from left, Kathleen, Vincent, and Norma enjoy a friendly dog's company. *Edna St. Vincent Millay Papers, Manuscript Division, Library of Congress, Washington, DC*

She also worked hard at school; she was eager to learn and outspoken in her questions. Her blunt and forthright attitude, however, irritated the principal, Frank Wilbur, who also taught history to Vincent's grade. He didn't like the way she seemed to challenge him in front of the other students. He had always thought it ridiculous that she was called Vincent, and finally, to express his irritation with her, he started calling her by other names that began with *V*—Violet, Veronica, Vivienne, Vanessa.

Vincent never rose to the bait. She always responded respectfully to his questions and politely corrected him as to her name. One day, in the middle of the first term, Mr. Wilbur's temper got the best of him, and he threw a book at Vincent, shouting that she had run the school long enough.

Vincent picked up the book, carried it to his desk, walked out of the classroom, and out of the school. Later that day Cora stormed into Mr. Wilbur's classroom, enraged at his treatment of her daughter. After she told him, in front of all of his students, exactly what she thought of him, he became so angry that he pushed her away from the door hard enough that she nearly fell down the stairs.

Cora's next trip, that same afternoon, was to the office of the school superintendent. They decided that Vincent should immediately leave the Elm Street School and enroll in Camden High School. Nobody was the least bit worried about her keeping up with the other freshmen.

Nearly a year younger than the others in her grade, Vincent took to high school with her usual enthusiasm and zeal. She made friends with the girls quickly, but some of the boys found her a little stuck-up, if not outright conceited. One of them, Raymond Tibbets, remembered that she was "a scrawny girl . . . and too smart for most of us. She hadn't learned, as many brilliant women do, to conceal her superior gifts from young male clods."

That first year, the school paper, the *Megunticook*, published Vincent's personal essay entitled "The Newest Freshman," about her experience as exactly that. (Unfortunately, the paper misspelled her last name as "Milley.")

Being published in the high school paper was a fine accomplishment, and felt good. But even better things came to Vincent that year. She was jubilant when *St. Nicholas* accepted her 18-line poem entitled "Forest Trees" and ran it in the October 1906 issue. The poem ended with these lines:

Around you all is changed—where now is land
Swift vessels ploughed to foam the seething main;
Kingdoms have risen, and the fire-fiend's hand
Has crushed them to their Mother Earth again;
And through it all ye stand, and still will stand
Till ages yet to come have owned your reign.

Less than six months later, in March 1907, *St. Nicholas* published another, much longer poem of hers. This one was called "The Land of Romance," and Vincent had composed it for a competition the magazine's editors established that assigned the length and title of the poems to be submitted. Vincent wrote in the first person about a child looking for romance, leaving it unclear whether the speaker of the poem was a girl or boy.

Show me the road to Romance! I cried, and
    he raised his head;
I know not the road to Romance, child. 'Tis a
    warm, bright way,'
he said.
And I trod it once with one whom I loved—
    with one who is long since dead.

A fairy child finally shows the human child the way to Romance in the closing stanza.

In the hush of the dying day,
The mossy walls and ivy towers of the land of
    Romance lay.
The breath of dying lilies haunted the twilight
    air
And the sob of a dreaming violin filled the
    silence everywhere.

"The Land of Romance" was Vincent's first big success. She won the St. Nicholas League's gold medal for the competition, and an editorial in the same issue praised her writing. The local newspaper, the *Camden*

Herald, reprinted the poem, and even Edward Wheeler, the editor of a New York–based publication called *Current Literature*, ran the impassioned poem in the April issue, remarking that he didn't know whether the writer was a girl or boy, but that "the poem . . . seems to us to be phenomenal."

Vincent's poems were remarkable for a girl her age. They were clearly influenced by the celebrated writers of the 19th century in whose works she had steeped herself throughout her childhood, writers read more often by adults than by children. They were poets like the Americans Henry Wadsworth Longfellow and Oliver Wendell Holmes and the English William Wordsworth and Alfred, Lord Tennyson. Cora loved these writers, and she had shared their poems with Vincent since before the girl herself could read. Vincent often acknowledged, later in her life, that it was her mother who had instilled in her both a love of language and an ear for it.

It was a wonderful spring for Vincent the year she turned 15. Not only did she receive literary acclaim, she won a role in the melodrama *Triss, or Beyond the Rockies*. The play was put on by the Camden Opera House, a 19th-century, three-story-high brick theater on the corner of Elm and Washington Streets, about a mile from her home.

"I am going to play Susie in Tris," she wrote in the diary—her first—that she began that March. "I have the stage all to myself for a while and I have a love scene with the villain. The villain is great."

Getting the role felt like compensation for Cora again being out of town, this time in Rockport on a consumption case. Wonderful as it was to be acting, playing piano, and writing, there was no escaping the relentless burden of housework. "How I hate to have her go!" Vincent complained to her diary. "Have to keep house all through vacation."

With rehearsals underway, she felt confident. "My part is going to be great—at least they all told me how well I did," she wrote. "I am awfully glad for this will be my first appearance. I want to make it a dazzling one."

The play was a hit, according to Vincent's diary, and she was especially proud of her performance. "*Triss* went off even better than I had expected," she boasted, "and we are going to Rockland as I had hoped. Everyone says that it is the best home talent performance ever given here, and a great many consider it better than the production of the traveling companies. I have received many congratulations on my acting of Susie Smith. My part isn't very large, but it is important and rather hard."

Her second year of high school coming to an end, Vincent was nearly bursting with dreams and desires. She had tasted success—she was a published, praised poet and an acclaimed actress—and she wanted more of it. Simultaneously weighed down by the household responsibilities forced by Cora's frequent absences and flying high with the heady emotions of being acknowledged as an artist, she was hungry for greater creative experiences. She wanted to hurl herself at the coming years, abandon the chores, and find the life she was meant to live. But she had two more years of high school before her, and she had no idea how to think any further ahead than that.

A Person of Intense Moods

1907–1909

By the time she was 16, Vincent had written 40 poems that she considered good enough to preserve. She copied them into a brown notebook, which she titled "Poetical Works of Vincent Millay." In the back she made an alphabetical listing of the poems' titles, and next to each title she noted how old she had been when she wrote the poem. The first poem she copied into the notebook was the award-winning "The Land of Romance" that had been published soon after her 15th birthday.

The subjects of Vincent's early teenage poems are like those often found in young people's writings. Some are filled with the loneliness many of us feel at that age;

in others she mourns lost loves (most likely more imagined than real) and exults in the beauty of nature's sea-
sons. The themes of "The Land of Romance" continue
in poems filled with fairies and moonbeams. Several are
written to her mother, to whom she gave the completed
volume of 61 poems in July 1908.

In one of the simpler, shorter ones, she promises to
always protect her mother from loneliness. The poem is
called "Song" and reads as though Vincent understood
that however deeply she and her sisters missed their
mother when she was away from them, it was probably
even more difficult for her mother, who suffered alone.

> *Dearest, when you go away*
> *My heart will go, too,*
> *Will be with you all the day,*
> *All the night with you.*
> *Where you are through lonely years,*
> *There my heart will be,*
> *I will guide you past all fears*
> *And bring you back to me.*

She dedicated the volume to her, as well: "To My
Mother, Whose interest and understanding have been
the life of many of these works and the inspiration of
many more, I lovingly dedicate this little volume. /
E.V.M. / July 10, 1908."

Serious as she was about her poetry, Vincent also
continued to find great joy in acting, piano playing, and

her friendships. After her success as Susie Smith in *Triss* in the spring of 1907, she won the lead in the Camden Opera House's production of *Gypsy the Mountain Waif*, which opened on December 6, 1907. Vincent's exuberant approach to life found its natural outlet in the world of the theater. And her quick and sharp memory, honed by years of memorizing poetry and musical compositions, made it easy for her to learn and remember her lines.

At Camden High School, it was still the girls who flocked around her, delighting in her high spirits and quick wit. One friend, Martha Knight, described Vincent as having "lots of spark and spunk; she fairly snapped"— maybe too much for the Camden adolescent boys. Another high school friend, Jessie Hosmer, remembered that she was "the life of the party, wherever she went." When Stella Derry's mother would ask why she avoided household tasks at home but liked to wash dishes and make potato stew at the Millays', Stella told her that it was because "Vincent made everything wonderful fun. She was always making up songs and games, and on walks she would make birds and plants and wild flowers as fascinating as people," although, Stella noted, "she could be a spitfire if she thought something wasn't fair."

When Cora was due home from one of her jobs, word quickly got around, and both boys and girls assembled to help with the cleaning. The boys beat the rugs and did the heavy cleaning, while the girls washed dishes and did the lighter work. It took at least six girls to do the dishes—two washing and four drying—because dishes were never washed until there wasn't a clean one left. Everybody sang as they cleaned, usually a song of Vincent's composition.

Helen Follett remembered that "the spirit of the house was one of freedom, friendliness, live and let live." Helen was Kathleen's pal and companion, but she went to Norma, who "was like a cheery flame among us," when she needed a confidante. Vincent was changeable: "haughty duchess one minute and the best of companions the next . . . she was a person of intense moods, and the house moved at her tempo."

Most of Vincent's friends came from two clubs she was part of: the Huckleberry Finners, a reading group, and the Genethod, a girls' Bible study group at the white-steepled Congregational Church on Elm Street that Vincent and her family attended every Sunday (though they always arrived late). The Genethod—the Welsh word for "daughter"—had been founded by Abbie Huston Evans, daughter of the pastor, the Welsh-born Bard Lewis Darenydd Evans. Even though Abbie was 11 years older than Vincent, she was one of her closest friends. In addition to teaching Sunday school, Abbie, too, wrote poetry and went on to become a well-regarded poet.

Even though Vincent attended services regularly and participated in the Genethod with Abbie, Stella, and other good friends like sisters Martha and Ethel Knight and Corinne Sawyer, Vincent was not a religious Christian in the traditional sense. "My God is all gods in one," she wrote in her diary on June 28, 1908. "When I see a beautiful sunset, I worship the god of Nature; when I see a hidden action brought to light, I worship the god of Truth; when I see a bad man punished and a good man go free, I worship the god of Justice; when I see a penitent forgiven, I worship the god of Mercy."

She especially found God in the profound natural beauty that made her feel as though her soul was ready to burst out of her. Her prayers were the poems she would write in praise of the earth, poems like "God's World," which was published in her first collection in 1917, in which she proclaimed,

> *Here such a passion is*
> *As stretcheth me apart,—Lord, I do fear*
> *Thou'st made the world too beautiful this year;*
> *My soul is all but out of me*

Vincent didn't write in her diary regularly, unlike her friend Ethel Knight (who first suggested to her that she keep one). Vincent usually turned to hers when her emotions threatened to overcome her. The day after penning the words about her religious beliefs, she confessed, "I guess I'm going to explode. I know just how a volcano feels before an eruption. Mama is so cross she can't look straight; Norma's got the only decent rocking chair in the house (which happens to be mine); and Kathleen is so unnaturally good that you keep thinking she must be sick. I suppose this is an awful tirade to deliver. . . . But it is very hard to be sixteen and the oldest of three."

Vincent's spirits brightened when Cora, who had brought home a little more money than usual, planned a delicious picnic for the girls for the next day. The sisters and their friends sat in the sunshine and gorged on salmon and sardine sandwiches and bananas, then indulged their sweet tooth with cookies, strawberry shortcake, and even chocolate.

"Such a lovely day as we had and such a lovely time," Vincent wrote in her diary that night. "The supper under the trees was such fun with the little cool breeze and the tiny new moon coming out for us to play by." They played a game that the sisters had made up, which they called "Rain Bow." Several girls ran through the meadow, hidden by the high grass, waving long silk ribbons of different colors above their heads. Seeing only the swirling ribbons, the others tried to guess who held which color ribbon. Later Vincent and Ethel "tried to skip off upstairs so I could read her part of my diary and just as we were getting interested, Martha and Norma and all the rest burst into the room and dragged us out."

Most often, though, the Millay sisters and their friends enjoyed summer activities that didn't cost any money—nature walks in the Camden Hills, canoe trips on Lake Megunticook, taking somebody's rowboat out into Penobscot Bay, or swimming in its bracingly cold water. Vincent collected wildflowers and pressed them into a scrapbook in which she also kept snapshots, programs from the Huckleberry Finners, the Genethod, and dramatic performances and piano concerts. She named the scrapbook "Rosemary" (thinking, maybe, of Ophelia in Shakespeare's *Hamlet*, when she says, "There's rosemary, that's for remembrance").

The scrapbook also held the postcards from the St. Nicholas League accepting Vincent's poems for publication, but it was to her diary that Vincent confided the depth of her feelings about her writing. "I've written so many verses and keep on writing so many more, that I became afraid that if I didn't write them into one big book I might forget some of them. . . . I love my verses so that it would be like taking my heart out if I should wake up some morning and find that all I could remember of one of my most loved—was the name."

One Sunday evening in July, having spent much of the day writing in the diary, she turned it into a character, one with a name, someone to fill the shoes of the mother who was so rarely home to listen and comfort. "I think I'll call her Ole Mammy Hush-Chile, she's so nice and cuddly and story-telly when you're all full of troubles and worries and little vexations."

That summer Vincent also started writing a novel. Like many writers whose first books are thinly disguised autobiographies, she wrote about a family of three sisters and their mother (there is no father in the book). "The Dear Incorrigibles" stars Katharine Randolph and her younger sisters, Margaret and Helen. In the opening scene, the mother is called away to take care of a relative suddenly taken ill and frets about leaving her daughters on their own. Katharine responds reassuringly. "'Now,

Muvver,' she said cheerfully. 'There's not a thing that I can see to scowl about. . . . Imagine a great big sixteen-year-old girl like me not being big enough to keep house for a little while.'"

Mrs. Randolph disappears for the balance of the book, which Vincent never finished. But in the few chapters she did write, in which the girls swim and playfully argue, she is clearly revising the life of the Millay family into a preferable version. In "The Dear Incorrigibles" the girls are alone not because their mother needs to earn an income as a paid nurse but because she is kindly caring for a sick family member.

When her senior year started, Vincent plunged head-long into the demands and opportunities of school life. She was editor of the school newspaper, had her first piano recital, and performed in every school play produced that year—and in three at the Camden Opera House. One of her classmates, handsome, dark-haired George Frochock, the Baptist minister's son and captain of the football team, played opposite her in *The Brookdale Mystery.*

In November, after four years in the ever more run-down, ever colder little house at the far end of Washington Street, Cora moved her family into the center of town to a ground-floor apartment at 40 Chestnut Street. Although two families lived in the apartments overhead, the house was right by the water and opposite the village green, which Vincent would cross to make the short walk to the Camden Opera House for rehearsals

This dreamy-eyed portrait of Vincent was taken sometime during her high school years. *Edna St. Vincent Millay Papers, Archives and Special Collections, Vassar College Libraries*

and performances. The sisters' bedroom window faced the harbor. Though not much larger than their home on Washington Street, it was much more comfortable and convenient.

In spite of Vincent's successes—or, more likely, because of them—most of the boys at Camden High, especially the 12 boys in her senior class, still didn't like her, finding her haughty and arrogant. Led by George Frochock, they ganged up against her, mimicking her when she read aloud from the psalms or the daily calendar at morning exercises, or stamping their feet and making catcalls while she was speaking. These small mockeries didn't bother Vincent; she was confident in her talents and protected by the love of her mother and sisters, as well as her strong friendships.

She even invited one of the boys, Henry Hall, to submit a poem for the *Megunticook*, now that she was editor in chief. She couldn't possibly have predicted that her invitation would have such an unfortunate outcome. She explained what happened to her diary, Mammy Hush-Chile, in one of only two entries she wrote during 1909.

"There is a boy in my class who, when we were Juniors, used to amuse himself by writing to me queer rhymes, meter-less things which I supposed he meant for poems. This year I was . . . at a loss for material for one of the issues and someone suggested that he write a poem. I thought that perhaps with care he might produce some funny verses. But when it was almost time for the material to come in he came to me and said that he had it partly done and could not possibly finish it. So I, about crazy for my paper, took the thing, finished it, changed it all over, rhymed lines that didn't rhyme, balanced the shaky meter of other lines, named the thing and had him sign his name to it."

Her good deed backfired in a devastating way. When everyone admired the poem, Vincent did not take credit for it, thinking Henry would have the integrity to admit what had occurred. Instead, Henry let everybody think he had indeed written it. As a result, when the time came for the seniors to elect the class poet, Vincent was nominated—but so was Henry Hall.

Vincent, dignified on the outside but inwardly heartbroken, withdrew her nomination, knowing the boys (who made up the majority of the class) would all vote

for Henry. She wasn't going to suffer the indignity of losing to a boy who, as she wrote to Mammy, "didn't have
stiffening enough in his great fat sluggish stolidity to get
to his feet and tell them that the only poem he ever had
printed in his life had been half written, wholly made
over, and published by me. *Oh*, it makes me white when
I think that it was my own fault. And I did it just for the
paper."

Vincent felt like it was the worst thing that had ever
happened to her. She was a famous local poet, the first
person in the region to be nationally recognized as a
poet, and even more important to her, her entire identity—both publicly and in her deepest core—was about
being a poet. Her feelings toward Henry spun out of
control. "I've helped him take away from me the only
thing I cared anything about, and now . . . I despise him
as I despise a snake. . . . I hate the sight of his fat white
hand,—his pretty, ladylike white hand, that copied and
copied in the symmetrical, self-satisfied writing that
stole my poem, my class poem that belonged to me."

The event sunk her into a depression so deep that she
stopped going to school. Vincent wouldn't confide in her
mother, but Cora understood how serious a blow had hit
Vincent's sensitive spirit. Looking for a way to revive her
daughter's spirits and confidence, Cora asked the school
principal if the essays being submitted for the class prize
could be written in prose or verse. She knew Vincent had
been working on a special poem called "La Joie de Vivre"
("The Joy of Life"). When the principal acknowledged

that verse was acceptable, Cora encouraged Vincent to complete the poem as her submission for the class prize.

The prospect of writing poetry again—and for a public competition—brought Vincent back to life. She threw herself into the poem, and returned to school before the end of the year. She attended the graduation exercises, which were held on June 16, 1909, in the place where Vincent had experienced previous triumphs: the Camden Opera House. The seniors made their presentations. Martha Knight opened with her essay on Scottish folklore. Stella Derry played a piano solo. The boys gave their speeches on ponderous topics such as "The Value of Higher Education" and "The Uses and Values of Electricity." (Fittingly, at the end Henry Hall stumbled over his class poem, "Our Destiny.")

When Vincent's turn came, midway through the program, she stood with poise, chin lifted, on the stage where she felt so very much at home. She wore a white lawn dress made by her aunt Sue; her red hair shone under the stage lights. The words poured forth like a deep-throated song:

> *The world and I are young!*
> *Never on lips of man*
> *Never since time began*
> *Has gladder song been sung.*

Vincent won the class prize, and with it not only the return of her confidence and reputation but also—an especially delicious icing on the cake—a $10 award. Her high school career ended in triumph.

Even with such a glorious finish to school, Vincent couldn't picture her future. For a girl from a poor family in rural Maine in 1909, no matter how talented and determined she might be, it was hard—almost

The Camden High School class of 1909, shown just before commencement, included Vincent, front row, third from left; her good friends Stella Derry on her left, Corinne Sawyer on her right, and Martha Knight next to Corinne; and annoying George Frochock, standing at far left. *Edna St. Vincent Millay Papers, Manuscript Division, Library of Congress, Washington, DC*

impossible—to create a future outside the boundaries of small-town life. Abbie was off to Radcliffe College thanks to a scholarship; she made Vincent promise to run the Sunday school in her absence. Vincent knew she would always write poetry, and she hoped to continue acting at the Camden Opera House. Otherwise, being done with school simply meant more time for household chores. At 17, Vincent prepared to become her family's housekeeper. Her heart and mind, however, yearned ever more desperately for a bigger world.

The railroad track is miles away,
And the day is loud with voices speaking,
Yet there isn't a train goes by all day
But I hear its whistle shrieking.

All night there isn't a train goes by,
Though the night is still for sleep and dreaming,
But I see its cinders red on the sky,
And hear its engine steaming.

My heart is warm with the friends I make,
And better friends I'll not be knowing;
But there isn't a train I wouldn't take,
No matter where it's going.

—*Travel, from* Second April, *1921*

Good-bye to Girlhood

1909–1911

Thanks to her cash award for the class prize, Vincent made plans to visit relatives in Newburyport, Massachusetts, where she and Norma had spent some happy weeks the previous summer. This time Vincent was on her own—just barely making the train out of Camden—and letters flowed regularly between the sisters, as well as between Vincent and Cora.

"I'm here!" she wrote Norma on July 16. "I've been all this time catching my breath. Wasn't that a lucky run? I do hope you haven't worried, but of course you have, just to keep in practice." After complaining of the heat ("hotter than it would be in the Sahara Desert if all the sand were cayenne pepper") she signed herself, "your angel child, Vincent."

Norma, in turn, wrote about the money she was earning babysitting and at other jobs, and that their father had sent five dollars just in time for rent day, "and we payed [sic] on the dot. He says he sent you some chink for ice cream and car rides. How much did he send you?" Kathleen, in her letters, complained about being home alone too much, but rejoiced about getting "two or three free rides on the merry-go-round a day."

While Vincent focused on the good times in her letters, she confessed to Mammy Hush-Chile when she returned to Camden in late September that her summer had not been all fun and games. "Of course I had a splendid time but I was glad to get home. Aunt Clem almost drove me crazy . . . being told when I shall or shall not change my dress . . . and when I shall not mail a letter." Her independent spirit had chafed under the unfamiliar scrutiny.

Waiting at home for Vincent was a silver badge from *St. Nicholas* for her poem "Young Mother Hubbard," which had appeared in the August 1909 issue. Soon after that honor came another: a professional traveling theater company, which cast a few of its roles locally, cast her in a play called *Willowdale*. Vincent was thrilled to be onstage again, and she was a huge hit in the lead role of Milly. Norma and Kathleen were also cast, in smaller roles. After its run in Camden, the company moved on to the town of Fairfield, where the new Milly suddenly fell ill. The director appealed to Vincent: would she make the 50-mile trip to take over the role?

Elated, she caught a train to Fairfield and arrived at the theater 20 minutes before the curtain. The other cast members rushed to help her, Vincent reported in her diary. "One hooked me up the back and pinned me together in a dozen places, one knelt and put on my shoes while I balanced with my hand on her shoulder, one went to find the frilly sun-bonnet I was to carry on in the first act."

Vincent loved being the center of attention, but even more exhilarating than her reception was being onstage again. She still knew all the lines, and she gave this performance everything she had. "And at the end," her diary entry concluded, "they gave me such a hand as I had never had before."

When the excitement of the play was over, Vincent found herself stuck in her new routine. Since she was home to keep house, Cora was traveling even more. Cooking, washing, sewing, embroidering, and paying calls on neighbors (who sometimes gave the Millays vegetables from their gardens) took up most of 17-year-old Vincent's time and energy. She took over Abbie's Sunday school class at the Congregational Church. Every Thursday was piano-lesson day with Mrs. French. (John Tufts had died in 1908.) In between all her obligations, she practiced her music and wrote poems as much as she could.

Although Norma was still in school, she had a job that winter, which meant more money for the family but also more demands on Vincent. She began a December

1909 letter to Cora saying, "I have only a few minutes for I have to get supper, for Norma is working in the 5 & 10 cent store and has to have her meals on time." Vincent fell ill on a regular basis (maybe due to her workload), and she would take to her bed for several days. If she was lucky, Cora would be home to nurse her; if not, her sisters did what they could.

That year Cora couldn't make it home for Christmas. Vincent sent her the new poem she was going to submit to *St. Nicholas*, entitled "Friends." In it, she explores the interior monologues of a girl and boy sitting together. He talks football as she sews.

He begins:

> *I've sat here all the afternoon,*
> *Watching her busy fingers send*
> *That needle in and out,—how soon*
> *I wonder, will she reach the end?*

While she begins: "He's sat here all the afternoon, / Talking about an awful game."

Each monologue finishes with a small but significant expression of their bond. He: "And I'll just have to let her sew, / Whether it's foolishness or not." She:

> *But Bob's a faithful friend to me,*
> *So let him talk that game detested*
> *And I will smile and seem to be*
> *Most wonderfully interested.*

The next April, Vincent would learn from her good friend Ethel Knight that this poem—the last she was able to submit to *St. Nicholas* since she was nearing the cutoff age of 18—had been awarded a five-dollar prize. While she had received other awards from the magazine, she had never won a cash prize. And money, of course, was always important to the Millays. "Words cannot express my feelings," Vincent noted in her diary. "I am simply crazed with delight." To add to her delight, the *Bangor World* wrote "a puff" about it, as did the *New Bedford Evening Standard* a few months later.

On her 18th birthday, February 22, 1910, Vincent was still tiny. Given her passion for the piano, her greatest despair was her small hands; her glove size was five and three-quarters. She also had improbably little feet—she wore size-two shoes. She hadn't entirely given up hope of growing; in March she pulled out an old green checked suit, which she had worn during her high school commencement season, and found it "disgracefully short. [It] gives me a tiny hope that I have grown since Commencement, a sixteenth of an inch would be gratefully received."

Music and poetry continued to vie for her devotion. In her diary she remarked one day that "Bach and I are getting acquainted and I find him very fascinating," and in another entry, "Read some of the Sonnets from the Portuguese, which are very beautiful especially to one who is acquainted with the Brownings [married poets Robert and Elizabeth Barrett Browning]."

But as serious as she was about the arts, Vincent was also a teenage girl with teenage interests: boys and clothes. At an April concert at the University of Maine she met Winthrop Wilson, a third-year student. She danced every dance (each with a different boy), and Winthrop brought her back to Camden at the end of the evening. She couldn't stop thinking about him and obsessed over the question of love, as millions of girls have done before and since, in her diary.

"Of course I'm not in love with him! It's ridiculous. But I think of him all the time and it makes me nervous . . . I've always expected it [love] to come but now that there seems a possibility of it I'm beginning to be afraid."

Then there were the seemingly magical clothes. "The devil is in the polka-dots on my flower satin dress," Vincent mused. "The first time I wore it was at a dance just before Frank Ryan went back to Connecticut . . . [with] my little tan pumps with the big silk bows. There is no doubt that they were bewitched. My tan silk stockings may have had something to do with it. There is something exhilarating about silk stockings."

And if attention to the arts, fashion, and romance didn't occupy her enough, later that spring Vincent was asked to teach Latin and ancient history at the high school while the regular teacher was out sick. She spent four days teaching freshmen and sophomores. While she found it funny to give instruction to "pupils as old and older than myself," she praised herself in her diary for not being "the least bit nervous."

Soon it was summer again. Small yellow flowering currants grew in clusters on bushes, and white clover and buttercups covered the grass. The air was filled with the droning of thick bumblebees. That year it was Cora's turn to visit her relatives in Newburyport, while the sisters stayed home and filled their days with dances, picnics, boating, and canoeing.

That summer Vincent discovered *The Rubáiyát of Omar Khayyám*, a collection of old Persian verses translated by the English poet Edward FitzGerald in the 19th century, known for its exhilarating mix of sensual delights and spirituality. (One of its most famous lines

Vincent (second from right) and her friends often enjoyed playful moments such as this in the beautiful Maine landscape. *Edna St. Vincent Millay Papers, Manuscript Division, Library of Congress, Washington, DC*

is "A jug of wine, a loaf of bread—and thou!") She spent much time with Russell Avery, a local boy who shared her ardor for the verses, and they read them to each other on boating trips and walks to the lily pond.

Overflowing with poetry, music, and love, Vincent spilled her mass of feelings into an old brown notebook, filling nine pages over two July days and titling it "Journal of a Little Girl Grown Up." It included emotional entries about leaving childhood behind, as well as drafts of poems in which she tried to define a new self, writing about herself in the third person:

> *Shall I not know, when we at last shall meet*
> *The wanton, wistful tread of her small feet?*
> *Her April eyes? Her smile, whose strange caress*
> *Is radiant with some secret tenderness?*
> *Her sweet nun-mouth behind its chastity*
> *Tense with the kisses that she keeps for me?*
> *Her voice? The autumn glory of her hair?*
> *Think you I would not know her anywhere?*

Vincent was also preparing for an August 3 solo piano recital in which she would play a couple of pieces, including Dvořák's "Humoresque." Some days before the recital, she and Russell had a falling out, and Vincent suffered one of her bouts of sickness, as well as the nuisance of six big warts. It was all enough to make her want her mother. She wrote Cora, "Am awfully homesick for you mother, and wish you'd come home before so very long, tho I don't want to cut your visit short, either." Within a week of receiving the letter, Cora was home—though she missed Vincent's recital.

When Halloween came, Ethel Knight gave a party for which Vincent made herself a witch costume. Describing it in her diary, she added a mysterious note: "I met my fate and everything is satisfactorily settled." Somebody photographed her in a field, Mount Battie in the

For a Halloween party in 1910, Vincent made what she described as "the dearest little witch costume." *Edna St. Vincent Millay Papers, Manuscript Division, Library of Congress, Washington, DC*

background, wearing the black robes and pointed hat, resting her chin and folded hands on a broomstick, bearing a thoughtful, somewhat troubled expression. Is she thinking about that fate, known only to her?

Almost 19, Vincent continued to berate herself for her haphazard diary keeping. On January 3, 1911, she grumbled, "I've tried to keep a diary and it doesn't work. I always forget it for two or three weeks. . . . This is to be more after the fashion of a journal. In a journal you can write whenever and whatever you please and it's nobody's business."

In April, though, Vincent turned Ole Mammy Hush-Chile upside down and went to the last page, where she began to write to a new, very secret confidant. "To you who, though yet but a shadow, are more real than reality to me: I consecrate myself. Confident that you are seeking for me even as I am waiting for you, I will fill the time until you come with preparation for you."

She was no longer writing to Ole Mammy Hush-Chile but to a boy—an imaginary boy, her true love. She arranged to "meet" him on the third of every month, at night, if she was alone in the house. She would light a candle, put on her prettiest nightgown, and pour out her heart to him in pages of hurried, increasingly slanted handwriting, the downstrokes plunging lower and lower with each new torrent of feeling.

After a few months of writing to her imaginary beloved, she turned back to Ole Mammy Hush-Chile and ended her relationship with the diary. "I have come to say goodbye. . . . I am very sad at parting with you, and doubly sad because it means and makes me realize that I am leaving my little-girlhood forever behind. Wish me Good-Luck, Mammy, in my big-girlhood."

On July 3 she devoted a new notebook to her imaginary love, titled "Vincent Millay—Her Book." Her first entry was a poem expressing her ever-growing frustration with the smallness of her daily life in Camden—the never-ending cleaning, washing, sewing, bread baking, keeping 14-year-old Kathleen and 17-year-old Norma in line, arguing with the grocer over the bill—and her craving for a bigger life filled with excitement and passion.

My life is but a seeking after life;
I live but in a great desire to live:
The undercurrent of my every thought:—
To seek you, find you, have you for my own
Who are my purpose and my destiny.
For me, the things that are do not exist;
The things that are for me are yet to be . . .

Her various writings reflect several sides of 19-year-old Vincent: the teasing high-spirited daughter, sister, and friend who kept house and went on picnics and boat rides; the secret passionate beloved of an imaginary boy; and the increasingly serious poet, grappling with questions of religion, faith, mortality, and the human condition. During the summer and autumn of 1911, she wrote a thoughtful "Essay on Faith" and worked on long, difficult poems that would eventually appear in her first published collection. These included "The Suicide" and "Interim," in which she writes:

> *There is your book, just as you laid it down,*
> *Face to the table,—I cannot believe*
> *That you are gone! . . .*
> *And here are the last words your fingers wrote,*
> *Scrawled in broad characters across a page*
> *In this brown book I gave you.*

Could Vincent have been writing another good-bye to her "little-girlhood" in these lines? If she began there, her thoughts grew much more complicated as the poem continues:

> *Not Truth, but Faith, it is*
> *That keeps the world alive. If all at once*
> *Faith were to slacken,—that unconscious faith*
> *Which must, I know, yet be the corner-stone*
> *Of all believing,—birds now flying fearless*
> *Across would drop in terror to the earth;*
> *Fishes would drown; and the all-governing reins*
> *Would tangle in the frantic hands of God*
> *And the world gallop headlong to destruction!*

The poems were solace for the increasing indignity and fatigue she felt from all the household work. "I'm getting old and ugly," she wrote in October. "My hands are stiff and rough and stained and blistered. I can feel my face dragging down. I can feel the lines coming underneath my skin."

Tired as she might feel that autumn, Vincent had started working on another poem, long, deeply thought-out, and different from all the others. It was the poem that would change Vincent's life.

The Poem That Raised a Furor

1912

In the early months of the freezing Maine winter of 1912, Vincent was in inner turmoil. She had been writing faithfully to her imaginary beloved on the third of every month—and sometimes in between—wild with love and need. In January she began to complain. She told him about her toothache and approaching cold, about her dissatisfaction "with everything,—myself first of all. . . . I suffer from inflammation of the imagination." Her handwriting grew more and more frantic as she wrote.

She was about to turn 20, and she was drowning in an ocean of emotion, feeling the intensities of pain and suffering, of joy and love, that had nothing to do with her own experiences. On February 11 she wrote in her diary,

"I do not think there is a woman in whom the roots of passion shoot deeper than in me . . . I feel intensely every little thing . . . the emotions I have not physically felt I have imagined so vividly as to make them real to me."

Vincent was trying to express this complicated torment in a poem. She had been working since the autumn and had 116 lines written, but she knew there was much more she needed to write. The poem opens simply, describing the view from Camden of mountains, woods, water, and islands:

> *All I could see from where I stood*
> *Was three long mountains and a wood;*
> *I turned and looked the other way,*
> *And saw three islands in a bay.*

Soon, though, the speaker has an astounding experience.

> *The sky, I thought, is not so grand;*
> *I 'most could touch it with my hand!*
> *And reaching up my hand to try,*
> *I screamed, to feel it touch the sky.*

> *I screamed, and—lo!—Infinity*
> *Came down and settled over me;*

The infinity of the universe brings her more knowledge than any human being can bear and, with it, immeasurable suffering. She "felt fierce fire / About a thousand people crawl; / Perished with each,—then mourned for all!"

> *A man was starving in Capri;*
> *He moved his eyes and looked at me;*
> *I felt his gaze, I heard his moan,*
> *And knew his hunger as my own.*

Longing for death as a relief from the pain and anguish, she "suffered death, but could not die"—until, finally, she sinks six feet underground. Grateful, she rests "deep in the earth . . . gladly dead," and hears the comforting sound of "the pitying rain."

Vincent had stopped writing there, with the poem's speaker buried alive. What could come after death? She played with some lines, but nothing seemed quite right.

On her 20th birthday, though, she seemed free of distress. "Good morning!" she wrote in her diary. "I am just twenty years old this minute. . . . Just think! Not in my teens anymore and never again. It seems so funny."

A week later Cora was working in Rockland and Norma and Kathleen were at school when a long-distance telephone call came in. It was from Kingman, Maine, where Henry Millay lived, and the operator's distant voice said, "Mr. Millay is very ill, and may not recover." Shocked, Vincent hung up and called her mother in Rockland. They decided that she should go to her father.

Getting to Kingman was no easy matter. Vincent took a chilly boat ride to Bucksport and then two trains. She stayed overnight in Bangor, with family friends. When she arrived in Kingman, her train was met by Ella Somerville, the daughter of Henry Millay's doctor. Vincent was to stay in the Somerville home, since her father rented a room in a boardinghouse. After she had dropped off her suitcase and had a cup of coffee, Vincent went with Dr. Somerville and Ella to the boardinghouse.

She hadn't seen her father since the day Cora made him leave home, 11 years earlier. When she entered the boardinghouse, she heard a man coughing upstairs and realized it was him. Would they be strangers to each other?

The boardinghouse owners—Mr. and Mrs. Boyd—and their sons, the private-duty nurse, Ella, and Dr. Somerville all watched Vincent carefully as she prepared to mount the stairs to her father's room. They advised her to stay calm, even though, as Vincent wrote in her diary, "I was not the least bit nervous and everybody else seemed very much upset. . . . Perhaps I wasn't so calm, tho, as I was numb."

Dr. Somerville let her enter the room alone, instructing her to stay only a few minutes. He reminded her that Henry did not have much time left.

"It didn't seem to me that the man on the bed was my father," she continued in her diary entry. She went over to him and said "Hello, papa, dear."

"When he heard me he opened his eyes—the bluest eyes I ever saw—and cried out 'Vincent! My little girl!' and struggled up in bed and held out his arms to me. . . . I put my arms around him and made him lie down again."

She talked to him—about nothing in particular—for a while, and then said she wished her eyes were blue, too, so that they would match her hat. "He whispered back—he couldn't speak at all—'You can't very well change your eyes, Vincent, but you might have got a green hat.'"

She laughed and he gave a small smile, his eyes closed. Vincent noticed that he had trouble keeping them open. She wrote her mother and sisters a quick postcard that night, saying she had "found Papa very low" and that Dr. Somerville had not given her much hope.

Perhaps it was her presence, or perhaps Henry was stronger than he appeared, but within days of Vincent's arrival his health began to improve. "He's had pneumonia, I guess," Vincent wrote Cora, "and asthma and a bad heart," but quickly she could send the happy news that "Papa is better and they think he will get well."

Now that her father was on the mend, Vincent enjoyed getting reacquainted with him. She visited him twice daily, reading to him for an hour or two, joking and singing (he thought she had "a voice with a future").

"I pop in and out all the time and we just love each other. Sometimes when I'm coming upstairs I call out, 'Hi papa!' like that, and sometimes I just say, 'I bet a cent my dad knows what's a-coming!' And then he'll laugh and tell me to hurry up."

She thoroughly enjoyed the freedom of her life in Kingman. She threw herself into the town's social life, attending shows and dances and thriving on 24-year-old Ella Somerville's adoring friendship. The two girls shared a love of poetry—Ella liked what Vincent called her "down under ground" poem-in-progress—and dancing, as well as a witty approach to life.

Ella had been instantly drawn to Vincent. From the day Vincent arrived, they shared a bed every night, talking, giggling, and laughing about the young men in Kingman. They also shared a crush on the violin player in the visiting Kickapoo-Laguna Vaudeville Medicine Show, which played in Kingman for a week. (Ella and Vincent went to every performance but one—when they had to attend a lecture.)

Vincent was having so much fun that she rarely wrote home, provoking concern in her sisters and Cora. They wrote often, asking for news and reminding Vincent how much she was needed at home. Finally Norma sent an angry note. "You have been up there almost three weeks and you haven't exerted yourself in writing letters to your family. . . . Just because you have found your father must you forget all about your mother and us kids? . . . I can't help scolding you for I am disgusted wif youse."

Vincent finally responded with a 15-page letter filled with reports on her social success and a detailed story of her flirtation with the violin player. The letter was full of Ella, too, and their attachment to each other. "Ella thinks she's going to die when I go home, but Doctor says that she'll live through it all right."

Not until she received Cora's letter written on March 21 did Vincent find a good reason to leave Kingman. Cora wrote about a poetry contest she had just learned of. The three best poems submitted by June 1 to the publisher Mitchell Kennerley in New York would receive large cash prizes. One hundred of them would be published in a collection to be titled *The Lyric Year*. Among the judges was Edward J. Wheeler, who had praised Vincent's "The Land of Romance" as "phenomenal" when it was published in *St. Nicholas* in March 1907. Cora reminded Vincent about Wheeler's praise in the letter and urged, "This seems to be a great chance for you. . . . Come home and make a good try."

Sorry to leave her charming father and the good times with Ella, Vincent returned to Camden. During her absence, Cora had found a new, brighter home for the family. They moved from the ground floor of 40 Chestnut Street to a two-story house at 82 Washington Street, across from the high school.

Heady from her social triumphs in Kingman, inspired by the possibility of a large cash prize, and her pulse quickened by a deadline, Vincent infused her "down under ground" poem with new energy. In less than two months she wrote the balance of 98 lines, in which the speaker reminisces heartbreakingly about the beauty of

In the spring of 1912 Cora and the girls moved into this house at 82 Washington Street. *Edna St. Vincent Millay Papers, Archives and Special Collections, Vassar College Libraries*

nature—"the fingers of the rain . . . the freshened, fragrant breeze / From drenched and dripping apple-trees, . . . the broad face of the sun . . . the multi-coloured multiform, / Belovèd beauty" of the sky—and is miraculously brought back to life.

I know not how such things can be!—
I breathed my soul back into me!

Ah! Up then from the ground sprang I
And hailed the earth with such a cry
As is not heard save from a man
Who has been dead, and lives again.
About the trees my arms I wound;
Like one gone mad I hugged the ground;
I raised my quivering arms on high;
I laughed and laughed into the sky;
Till at my throat a strangling sob
Caught fiercely, and a great heart-throb
Sent instant tears into my eyes:
O God, I cried, no dark disguise
Can e'er hereafter hide from me
Thy radiant identity!

Had Vincent's exhilarating stay in Kingman, her redis-
covery of her father, her passionate friendship with Ella,
all combined to make her feel reborn, risen from under
the weighty anguish of the previous months? Whatever
transpired within Vincent, she was able to compose a
214-line emotion-driven poem that compelled the reader
to keep reading: a page-turner. And all of it in rhyming
couplets.

She titled her poem "Renaissance" and got permission to type it up in the Camden High School office. On
May 27 she mailed it to the Mitchell Kennerley offices

on East 28th Street in New York City, along with three others ("La Joie de Vivre," "The Suicide," and "Interim"), each under separate cover. She signed each of the poems "E. Vincent Millay."

The poems submitted, Vincent turned her attention back to life in Camden. She sewed and baked for Norma's high school graduation festivities and prepared for several of her friends' upcoming weddings. She and Norma rehearsed duets to perform at the commencement ceremony, which would be in the opera house, just as Vincent's had been three years earlier.

On the afternoon of July 19, as Vincent approached home with a pail of blueberries she had picked for supper, she saw Cora waiting on the doorstep. As she came closer, her eyes spotted a letter in her mother's hand.

Vincent poses happily in front of the Washington Street house sometime in 1912.
Edna St. Vincent Millay Papers, Archives and Special Collections, Vassar College Libraries

The letter was addressed to E. Vincent Millay, Esq. It began "Dear Sir" and went on to say that "Renaissance" had been accepted as one of the best 100 poems in *The Lyric Year* competition. Asking for biographical information, the letter was signed, simply, "The Editor." What the letter did not say, however, was whether the poem had won a cash prize.

Vincent replied, introducing herself. "It may astonish you that I am no 'Esquire' at all, nor even a plain 'Mister'; in fact, that I am just an aspiring 'Miss' of twenty." She spilled forth details about her life, her early poems, her love of music and piano playing, her passion for *The Rubáiyát*. She even enclosed a photograph.

The editor, still anonymous, responded on August 6. "Dear and true Poetess! You have indeed astonished me through and through—a lassie o' twenty—is it possible? . . . Certainly I did not suspect that a fence-vaulting, Bach-mad, ninety-nine-pound mite of a girl was causing all the hubbub! Sometimes I think that *Renascence* is the most interesting poem in the selected Hundred of The Lyric Year." (The editors had changed the title from "Renaissance" to the English spelling, "Renascence.")

The editor still made no mention of the prize, but their flirtatious correspondence continued for months, growing ever more personal. Eventually he identified himself as Ferdinand Earle and began to hint strongly that Vincent was one of the prizewinners.

While Vincent was engaged in this exciting new relationship, Norma was working as a waitress at Camden's

Whitehall, a sprawling white hotel with wide front porches and columns, overlooking the bay. Built in 1834 as a sea captain's home, it had become a summer hotel for elite guests in 1901. Each year the staff put on a show for the guests at the end of the summer season, followed by a masquerade ball. Norma persuaded Vincent to perform.

Vincent won first prize for the Pierrette (a comedic stage character) costume Norma made for her: a short, full white skirt fitted at the waist, with a low-cut sleeveless bodice and black pom-poms down the front, and a black velvet mask with rosettes of red crepe paper. Norma won the prize for best dancer. Vincent played the piano and the girls sang. After the music, one of the

Whitehall still operates as a hotel in Camden, Maine, today. *Courtesy of Lark Hotels*

guests asked for a poem, and Vincent told them about her recent honor and the upcoming publication of "Renascence." Somebody asked her to recite it.

Still sitting at the piano, Vincent turned away from the audience of 40 guests, showing them only her profile. Her deep, resonant voice captivated the listeners, just as it had the night of her high school commencement. She recited the 214 lines to a spellbound silence. When she finished, the applause was stupendous. She was invited to return for an encore performance the next night.

One of the Whitehall guests that evening was Caroline Dow, dean of the YWCA Training School in New York City. She was astounded by Vincent's accomplished poem and by her mesmerizing performance. She had not expected to come upon anybody with such talent and stage presence in a small seaside town in Maine.

Convinced that Vincent should have the opportunity for higher education, Miss Dow visited Cora and Vincent and proposed to send the young poet to Vassar College, a women's school in Poughkeepsie, New York. She had several wealthy friends who, she believed, would want to sponsor the education of such a talented young woman. Cora and Vincent did not need to be persuaded.

Caroline Dow wasn't the only Whitehall guest who had that idea. Mrs. Julius Esselbourne had been equally impressed with Vincent and wanted to send her to Smith College, another women's school, this one in Northampton, Massachusetts. Suddenly Vincent was a desirable prize caught between two suitors.

She was still corresponding with Mr. Earle, who sent her some editing suggestions for "Renascence," which Vincent took to heart. He continued, he told her, to promote the poem for the first-place award.

After all his encouragement, Vincent was crushed, in early November, to learn that she had not won first prize. In fact, she had not won any of the cash prizes, only an honorable mention. She wrote furiously to Mr. Earle. "This, then, is what I have been waiting for, from day to day, from mail to mail, in such an agony as I had not known I could experience. This is the answer, this is the end. I wonder why I am not crying. My mother is crying. Did you ever hear your mother cry as if her heart would break? It is a strange and terrible sound. I think I shall never forget it."

When *The Lyric Year* was published late in 1912, public outrage erupted over the awards. The many famous writers included, such as Sara Teasdale, Louis Untermeyer, and Joyce Kilmer, denounced the editors for not awarding "Renascence" first prize. The first-prize winner, Orrick Johns, wrote later, "I realized it was an unmerited award. The outstanding poem in that book was 'Renascence' by Edna St. Vincent Millay, immediately acknowledged by every authoritative critic as such." He refused to attend the awards banquet. Supposedly one of the three top winners offered Vincent his cash prize, and she refused.

"Renascence" was praised in the *Chicago Post*, the *New York Times Book Review*, the *St. Louis Mirror*, and by the secretary of the Poetry Society of America, Jessie Ritten-house. She invited Vincent to give a reading, writing to Ferdinand Earle that "Renascence" was "the best thing in the book . . . in fact one of the freshest and most origi-nal things in modern poetry. If it doesn't get the prize, I pity your judges!" Copying all this into her diary, Vin-cent noted, "But it didn't get the prize! Everything but the money!"

By the end of 1912, Vincent was on the brink of two grand new adventures. She was, as one critic described her, "the young girl from Camden, Maine, who became famous through *not* receiving the prize." She was also a prospective college student, anxiously presenting her-self and her academic credentials to the two prestigious schools that wanted her. Both Smith and Vassar were woo-ing her with promises of tuition and all expenses paid. In the end, Vincent chose Vassar, attracted by the prospect of being one of the very few students from Maine.

Reviewing Vincent's high school transcript, which showed grades in the 90s for everything except algebra, the college administrators believed she nevertheless needed additional preparatory courses before starting college. Caroline Dow arranged for her to spend the spring semester at Barnard College in New York City as a special student before moving on to Vassar. Bar-nard dean Virginia Gildersleeve first wrote that "she should be admitted without entrance examinations . . . only if she has done some work of exceptional merit." After reading Vincent's poetry, though, she changed her mind. "Let us by all means have Miss Millay here, and handle her gently."

Vincent was unaware of all this. So she was greatly surprised to receive a telegram from Miss Dow on February 3, 1913, telling her to come to New York immediately to start her studies at Barnard.

On January 10 she had bid her imaginary love farewell. "Some people think I'm going to be a great poet," she wrote. "And I'm going to be sent to college so that I may have a chance to be great,—but I don't know— I'm afraid—afraid I'm too—too *little*, I guess, to be very much, after all. . . . It seems to me that all I am really good for is to love you."

She pricked her finger and put a "drop of red, red blood" into a small white box, along with the secret diary and the ring she wore when she met with her beloved. She sealed it with candle wax before blowing out the candle one last time. A few weeks later the young poet boarded the train for Manhattan.

Hello, New York!

Spring 1913

Early in the morning of February 5, 1913, Vincent arrived at Manhattan's newly renovated Grand Central Terminal. Disembarking from her sleeper car, she was among the early passengers to walk the beautiful new grand concourse, finished in marble and lined with elevated "kissing galleries," where travelers could make their greetings and farewells apart from the heavy traffic flow.

Into this grandeur she stepped, wearing her homemade brown suit with matching hat and ribbons in her pigtails, which vastly diminished the elegant effect she hoped to create. "Fancy! After all these years to strike New York in braids!" she wrote in her diary. She had

forgotten her hair combs at home. Caroline Dow had
sent an assistant, Mary Alice Finney, to meet her train.

Miss Finney bought the young poet (who looked about
12 years old to her) an ice cream soda, then took her to
the National Training School for the YWCA, where she
would live. Her room was just like all the others in the
building, except for one feature that enchanted Vincent.
She described it in a letter: "The hot water came out of
the cold water faucet . . . when I turned on the water for
the first time and found out about it I thought to myself,
'Well, here's where you belong,' it was that comfy. You
see the room was so absolutely perfect in every way that
you'd hardly believe anything like that could happen in
it. And every time it did, I'd grin. You see, one said 'Hot'
and the other said 'Cold,'—and they both were liars. It
was beautiful."

She'd been told to rest, but with New York City beck-
oning from eight floors below, rest was impossible. The
YWCA was on Lexington Avenue and 52nd Street, in the
heart of Manhattan. She looked out her window to see
"buildings everywhere . . . children on roller skates playing tag on the sidewalk, smokestacks *and* smokestacks,
windows and windows, and signs way up high on the
tops of factories and cars and taxicabs,—and *noise*, yes,
in New York you can *see* the noise."

She registered for her classes at Barnard College
uptown at 116th Street that afternoon. She had to take
two English classes and one each in French and Latin.

Vassar's dean, Ella McCaleb, hoped that these courses would bring Vincent up to the level of other freshmen entering the college in the autumn—at least in those subjects. Over the summer, in Camden, Vincent would have to prepare herself in algebra, ancient history, and further in Latin.

Her first week in Manhattan was a flurry: a concert at Carnegie Hall, a Broadway play, and navigating the subways on her own. Caroline Dow took her shopping, and Vincent sent home a delicious cataloging of her new wardrobe. She now owned "a pair of black satin pumps with eleven story heels . . . and big rhinestone buckles, white kid gloves, sixteen button length way up ones, and a scarf, a beautiful soft big white silk one with pale yellow roses in it." Those were just some of the accessories. Miss Dow also bought her numerous waists (garments similar to what we call blouses today), collars, linen handkerchiefs, a luxurious chinchilla coat, and other splendid items. She turned 21 in Manhattan but still looked like a teenager playing dress-up in her fancy new clothes.

Very soon after her arrival, Vincent began to be introduced to the literary lights of the city. With the success of "Renascence" still fresh, poets and publishers were eager to meet the girl whose poem had caused such a furor. She and the poet Sara Teasdale, who was eight years older, quickly became dear friends, sharing their poems with each other. She met Edward J. Wheeler, who apologized to her for not awarding "Renascence" one of the top three prizes, as well as her correspondent

Ferdinand Earle and another poet who would become a lifelong friend, Harold "Hal" Witter Bynner.

Hal and poet Arthur Davison Ficke had been reading *The Lyric Year* together when they stumbled upon "Renascence" and were convinced that the author's identity was a hoax. They insisted that the author had to be "a brawny male of forty-five." Vincent had responded with a flirtatious letter to Arthur and enclosed her photograph, starting yet another affectionate correspondence that turned into one of the most enduring, and important, relationships of her life.

Vincent threw herself into her studies at Barnard and continued composing new poems. Often she grew frustrated by the competing needs. Meaning to study, she was easily distracted by working on her poems. Or, settled into her studies, she lamented, "I am going crazy with the poems that I simply can't get time to write. It isn't a joke. I can't study now; I'm too old. I ought to be through college at my age, and I know it, and I have other things to think about and *I can't study.*"

Still the studying continued, and the poems came. She completed two poems she had started in Camden, "Journey" and "God's World." Both poems praise the natural world, and both were accepted for publication by Mitchell Kennerley's magazine, the *Forum*, in April. The publisher sent her a check for $25—the first money she had earned for her writing since *St. Nicholas*—and she was overjoyed. She sent it home to Cora, who gratefully paid off some old bills.

"Journey" appeared first, in the May issue, and "God's World," which Vincent believed "the better poem," soon after. In the latter, Vincent described the vivid beauty of autumn with the passion of someone in love:

> *Oh world, I cannot hold thee close enough!*
> *Thy winds, thy wide grey skies!*
> *Thy mists, that roll and rise!*
> *Thy woods, this autumn day*
> *That ache and sag*
> *and all but cry with colour!*

The intense emotion, helped by all the exclamation points, overcomes the formal language of the poem, with its "thys" and "thees," and makes the reader's heart ache with the poet's.

Often the allure of the city tore Vincent away from both her studies and her writing. She attended her first grand operas and went to art exhibitions, baseball games, and Poetry Society functions—including a party given in her honor on March 9. In April Vincent finally met her publisher, Mitchell Kennerley. He wanted to bring out a volume of her poetry, but Vincent objected. She knew she didn't have enough good poems for even a small volume.

Mr. Kennerley could wait. He extended another invitation. He and his wife, Helen, lived in a mansion in Mamaroneck, New York, a short train ride from the city, where they often held parties for the literary and artistic crowd. "He has invited me out some Sunday to see him and her and the kiddies!" Vincent wrote in her diary. "They are in the *country*!—I can eat grass!"

A month later she took the train to her first Kennerley party, where she met his cousin, a 40-year-old Englishman named Arthur Hooley, who was editor of the *Forum*. Under the pseudonym Charles Vale, he had written a rave review of "Renascence" in the magazine. It had appeared just weeks before Vincent's arrival in New York—and he was the one who had bought and published the two recent poems from Vincent. In spite of their age difference, they were immediately smitten with each other.

Vincent spent much of the following month traveling back and forth between Manhattan and Mamaroneck, spending every minute she could with Hooley before painfully ending what she knew was an unwise relationship. (He was not only older, he was maddeningly contradictory about his feelings for her.) While the brief romance may have ended, Arthur Hooley continued to publish Vincent's poems in the *Forum* for the next three years.

Her classes finished, Vincent returned to Camden in June. She had done just barely well enough during her semester at Barnard for Vassar to admit her. Vassar's Dean McCaleb wrote to Caroline Dow: "Miss Millay has perhaps told you that we have admitted her, although she is somewhat heavily conditioned."

Vincent corresponded frequently with Dean McCaleb that summer. "Yes, indeed, I'm coming!" she wrote her on July 7. "And I'm prepared for a whole lot of work this summer. . . . I wish you would forget all about that algebra. I hate algebra. You might just as well know it now. But I can do it if I have to; my little sister will help me. It's just like cat's cradle for her."

Both Vincent and Vassar's administrators looked ahead to September with some concern. Vincent asked Dean McCaleb, "I wonder if I ought to know just what to do without bothering you any more. I probably seem very stupid. Do all the girls know everything without asking?" Dean McCaleb responded kindly, while acknowledging that Vincent was an out-of-the-ordinary

"Supper Picnics" were popular with Vincent and her friends during the summer months. This one took place on Great Spruce Head Island, on Penobscot Bay; Vincent is in the middle row, third from left, while sister Kathleen is in the top row, third from left. *Edna St. Vincent Millay Papers, Manuscript Division, Library of Congress, Washington, DC*

incoming student and it was only natural that she should have many questions.

Vincent wasn't really worried. She had won over New York City's literary society that spring. Come September, she would win over Vassar's students and faculty, too.

The Pink-and-Gray College

1913–1917

Classes at Vassar began on September 22. Vincent was four years older than most of her fellow students in the class of 1917, but in spite of her classes at Barnard and her summer studies, she was not as well prepared academically as most of her classmates. Plus she was free-spirited, independent, and sometimes irreverent. Her history entrance exam—which she failed, along with the algebra exam—is just one example of her unconventional approach to her studies.

She began the history exam by writing, "I was prepared in American History: at my home in Camden, Maine, in the hammock, on the roof and behind the stove." Among the proclamations she made in the six handwritten pages is the statement that "the psychological cause of the Revolution was, as is the cause today of so many more interesting disturbances,—incompatibility." Her unusual exam closed with the following: "At precisely this point the pleasant lady in an Alice-blue coat, who I wish might be my instructor in History, requests us all to bring our papers to a close. As I know a great deal about American history which I haven't had a chance to say, I am sorry, but obedient."

The history instructor, C. Mildred Thompson, disagreed that Vincent knew a great deal about American history. She graded the paper 1- (basically failing her). Her German professor, Florence G. Jenney, though, characterized her as "an excellent student. . . . She gave her active attention to everything that was said. . . . She was always ready to assist in non-academic enterprises and to meet an emergency, as when a class song was needed in short order, or a program had to be improvised at the last minute."

The rules and restrictions at Vassar came as a shock to Vincent. She had not been brought up with rules, and she began to break them at once, smoking in the cemetery, cutting classes regularly, and leaving campus when she pleased, without permission. Many years later Professor Jenney recalled Vincent's explanation. "She could not take [the rules] seriously . . . [she] had led an independent life with no 'silly protection' such as the girls were given in the women's colleges; it was hard to realize that things her mother had always let her do were not allowed."

Vincent complained about Vassar in a letter that first autumn to her friend Arthur Davison Ficke, writing, "I hate this pink-and-gray college." Just a few months later, though, she was apologizing to Cora for not writing often enough because she was "getting so crazy about Vassar & so wrapped up in Vassar doings. . . . Oh, I love my college!"

Her changed feelings likely had to do with the attention she attracted from the other students. Fellow student Agnes Rogers recalled that "she was one of the celebrities. . . . She had done something. She was special. . . . She was luminous, as though there were a light behind her. . . . I felt it. Everybody did."

At the all-girls college, passionate friendships developed and broke apart over teas, luncheons, and dances. Vincent quickly gained an almost cultish following, and her letters to her family, as well as her diary entries, are full of the intricate relationships she was cultivating. That first fall, there was Catherine Filene—a "handsome quiet big child"—and Katharine Tilt, whose relationship with Vincent made Catherine jealous.

Vincent enjoyed playing her girlfriends against each other. Students took turns in pairs hosting teas in their rooms; when Vincent and Katharine hosted in early December and had an argument, Vincent made sure that Katharine saw her being consoled by Catherine.

Her relationships were not limited to her fellow students. She traveled back to Manhattan (often without permission) to socialize with the writers, editors, and others she had met the previous spring. After spending Christmas in Camden, she accepted an invitation to stay with the Kennerleys before returning to Vassar. On this Mamaroneck visit, she again encountered Arthur Hooley, as well as Hal Bynner. This time she found herself falling for Hal. She was leading a double life: one as a college girl and the other as an intriguing member of the New York literary scene.

For both lives, her need for nice clothes was relentless. She bought the dress of her dreams from Wanamaker's department store. "I have paid $10.50 for a tan linen, tailory, cutey, *so* becoming, with a white muslin collar, spring dress, that I really need, to wear to college," she wrote.

The world came to know that dress well after the celebrated photographer Arnold Genthe took her portrait wearing it in the spring of 1914. In the picture, she stands in profile below a magnolia tree on the Kennerleys' Mamaroneck property, the blossoming branches draped around her. It became the best-known image of the young poet.

Just before the end of her freshman year, Vincent won a $15 prize in the Miscellany Prize Contest for a poem she had written in September 1911, "Interim." Again she sent the money home to Cora. The award brought her increased admiration at Vassar. Still, as at Barnard, she struggled to balance her studies, social life, and writing, and professors noted her frequent absences from class.

Vincent at the Kennerleys' home in Mamaroneck, New York, in the spring of 1914. *Genthe Collection, Library of Congress Prints and Photographs Division, Washington, DC*

In the fall of her sophomore year, the *Forum* published two of her poems: "The Shroud" and "Sorrow," an exploration of what we now understand as depression.

Sorrow like a ceaseless rain
Beats upon my heart.
People twist and scream in pain,—
Dawn will find them still again.
This has neither wax nor wane,
Neither stop nor start.

People dress and go to town;
I sit in my chair.
All my thoughts are slow and brown:
Standing up or sitting down
Little matters, or what gown
Or what shoes I wear.

In her sophomore year, too, Vincent was able to indulge her love for performing onstage; she won the lead role in the Sophomore Party Play. She was to play the princess, and she was greatly excited by the honor. Clothed in a white satin dress she'd made herself, she was a huge success, lauded by students and faculty alike. It was the first of many triumphant performances for Vincent at Vassar. By the time she graduated in 1917, she had starred in seven plays.

Many of Vassar's productions drew professional reviewers from local newspapers, who never failed to single out Vincent's performances. When the college celebrated its 50th anniversary in October 1915 with an outdoor Pageant of Athena, Vincent played Marie de France, the first woman to write poetry in France, in the 12th century. The *Poughkeepsie Eagle* described her, gliding across the lawn toward the specially built open-air theater, as "slight and dainty even in a dress of white satin with a train so big that two pages were required to carry it. . . . Her grace was as great as her learning."

In October 1915 Vincent won great praise for her portrayal of Marie de France. *Edna St. Vincent Millay Papers, Archives and Special Collections, Vassar College Libraries*

Keeping up her pace, in May of her sophomore year Vincent wrote two musical compositions, "Druid's Chant" and "Song of the Nations," for Vassar's traditional Tree Ceremonies. These ceremonies, in which the class ritualistically plants a tree, had been held annually by the sophomore class since 1868. And Arthur Hooley published another of her poems, this one titled "Indifference," in the *Forum*.

Her intense relationships with fellow students flourished. Living in North Hall her sophomore year, she met junior Elaine Ralli, and the two girls quickly bonded, in spite of their differences. Vincent described Elaine to Norma: "hockey hero, cheer-leader, rides horseback a lot, very boyish & makes a lot of noise, not tall, but all muscle. . . . She's just naturally taken me, for better or for worse, and Lord knows why."

Vincent spent Thanksgiving with the Rallis, who were a wealthy family, in their luxurious Manhattan apartment, and visited again before returning to Camden for Christmas. The young women didn't want to be parted for the summer, so Elaine invited herself to Camden. Her mother wrote Cora, offering to pay for her upkeep, and Cora happily accepted.

Vincent, eager that her family make a good first impression, nervously prepared them for Elaine's arrival, sending a long list of instructions, including how they each should look ("your hair all *simple*, Non, not frizzed & false. You see at college, no one ever *hears* of false hair.") and how the house should smell ("Burn something so it will smell all *homey*, coffee or a cigarette, you know"). Elaine stayed most of the summer, enjoying Camden activities like sailing, swimming, and hiking. Soon after she left, Vincent followed Elaine down to her family's summer home in Bellport, Long Island, for more fun together.

The friendship continued into the next academic year, but Vincent began to divide her time between Elaine and other girls, especially Isobel Simpson, a Greek major with whom Vincent shared a deep interest in the Greek and Latin poets. Elaine was not happy at the change in their friendship. "Dearest little old sweetheart—miss you dear—Gee!" she wrote her before Christmas. But Vincent, encouraged by Caroline Dow, had decided she needed to expand her circle of friends, and so she did.

Important as her friendships were to her, Vincent's poetry took first place in her heart. Throughout her years at Vassar, her poems consistently won praise and publication. In the spring of 1916 she won the Intercollegiate Prize for the 138-line poem entitled "The Suicide," which she had started five years earlier, in Camden, during the difficult summer of 1911. It begins with a furious rant: "Curse thee, Life, I will live with thee no more! / Thou hast mocked me, starved me, beat my body sore! / And all for a pledge that was not pledged by me." Like "Renascence," "The Suicide" traces a radical change of spirit, including a stay in heaven that becomes intolerable to the poem's speaker.

Vincent had returned to work on "The Suicide" at Vassar, in spite of a lack of encouragement from Caroline

Dow and others. Not only did the poem win the prize, it was also reviewed by the literary critic Edmund Wilson in the *New York Evening Sun* and praised for "frankness, intensity and dramatic feeling."

Mitchell Kennerley published it along with two others that spring, "Witch-Wife," a lighthearted declaration that whatever her passions and pleasures, at heart the subject of the poem belongs only to herself, and "Blue-Beard," inspired by an ancient folktale about a wicked king, a locked door, and a forbidden chamber. The sonnet chastises the listener for intruding on the poet's private self.

> *Yet this alone out of my life I kept*
> *Unto myself, lest any know me quite;*
> *And you did so profane me when you crept*
> *Unto the threshold of this room tonight*
> *That I must never more behold your face.*
> *This now is yours. I seek another place.*

Vincent sailed through her senior year with her usual zest, writing poems and performing in plays. She also wrote the words and music for the Baccalaureate Hymn, which was to be sung during the June 10 Baccalaureate Service at Vassar's 1917 commencement ceremonies.

But Vassar's most famous student nearly did not graduate. Her continuous disregard for the college's rules finally caught up with her a few weeks before commencement.

Vincent felt in her element at Vassar, as evidenced by her happy expression in this 1917 photo taken at the college. *Edna St. Vincent Millay Papers, Archives and Special Collections, Vassar College Libraries*

Earlier in the spring she had been invited to the opera in Manhattan and stayed overnight, even though she knew she shouldn't. As punishment, she was "campused"—meaning she was not allowed to spend any more nights away from Vassar. One Saturday in May she and her roommate Charlotte Babcock were studying when two friends, Gertrude Bruyn and Winifred Fuller, showed up in an exciting vehicle—a Saxon roadster. They invited Charlotte to go for a ride and persuaded Vincent to come along.

The girls picked up sandwiches and started off for the countryside. Decades later, Charlotte recounted the weekend in a letter to the editor of Vassar's alumnae magazine. "We drove around . . . Vincent composing verses about the cherry trees and peach trees then in radiant bloom, and I wrote my fiancé late that night 'we talked and sang and just yelled for joy as we skipped along up hill and down dale in the blessed little Saxon.'"

The girls accepted the Bruyns' invitation to stay overnight, and Charlotte telephoned one of their roommates to let her know. The girls enjoyed supper, took in a movie, then returned to the house to play piano and sing. The next day Gertrude drove them around, and they made a stop at the Watson Hollow Inn. Charlotte notes, "I don't remember whether or not we all signed our names in the guest book, but Edna St. Vincent Millay did, and, it is said, after a man's!"

Nothing would have come of the adventure, except that a few days later a Vassar warden, responsible for enforcing the college's rules, stopped into the Watson Hollow Inn for lunch. She saw Vincent's name in the guest book and brought the news back to Vassar. For such a major infringement, the faculty voted to suspend Vincent from college indefinitely. After four years as a Vassar celebrity, Vincent would not be allowed to graduate. She would have her degree, but it would be mailed to her.

The campus exploded in fury. Nearly half of the seniors presented a petition requesting Vincent be allowed to graduate with her class. The petition had 108 signatures and was accompanied by 18 letters urging that the penalty was too severe.

Even Cora wrote to Dean McCaleb and Vassar's president, Dr. Henry Noble MacCracken. She thanked Vassar for the great opportunity the college had given Vincent but urged them to reconsider their decision to exclude her from the commencement ceremony. When Dean McCaleb wrote back, she reminded Cora that "all the way through college Vincent has found it extremely difficult to live according to college regulations, and she has been forgiven possibly too often."

Yet, she was forgiven one more time. The faculty relented and voted to end Vincent's suspension the night before commencement. She was allowed to graduate with her class on June 12. At the age of 25, college degree in hand, Vincent was free to pursue an independent life.

The "It Girl" of Greenwich Village

1917–1921

Just days after commencement, Vincent headed to New York City to look for work. Her plan was to support her poetry writing with acting jobs. But after only a week, she decided it would be smarter to return to Camden for the summer. She planned to mend and make over her clothes and do some writing, which she hoped would sell. In a letter to Norma, she daydreamed about sharing a room with her in the city come winter. Her only worry was leaving their mother alone in Camden.

Vincent would travel home with Kathleen, who had been taken up by Caroline Dow a few years earlier, just as Vincent had been. Kathleen was graduating from the Hartridge School in nearby Plainfield, New Jersey, in preparation for Vassar. Vincent requested Norma make baked beans for their Saturday night reunion supper.

She didn't write many poems that summer, but three earlier ones were published in the August 1917 issue of *Poetry* magazine: "Kin to Sorrow," "A Little Tavern," and "Afternoon on a Hill." By autumn she was back in New York, after a stay in Connecticut with some new, important theater friends, actor-playwright Charles Rann Kennedy and his wife, actress and acting coach Edith Wynne Matthison. The couple had seen Vincent perform in one of her own plays at Vassar and had been much impressed. Visiting her backstage, they had promised to help her acting career—they had many powerful friends and connections in the theater world and vowed to help her secure auditions.

Her visit with the Kennedys was "oh, *wonderful!*" as she wrote her family. She studied acting technique with Edith and was growing more confident that she would soon be employed as an actress. She also worked on writing new poems and prepared the manuscript for her first volume of poetry for Mitchell Kennerley. She finally felt she had enough good work to publish a book, and he wanted to bring it out in December.

Inspired by the upcoming publication of her book, the Kennedys, as well as Caroline Dow, Elizabeth Haight, and one of Haight's wealthy friends, Blanche Hooker, were booking poetry readings for Vincent in homes, schools, and theaters. For some she would earn as much as $50.

One of her first readings was at Blanche Hooker's home in Greenwich, Connecticut, on September 17. It was at this reading that Vincent accidentally hit upon what would become her signature style for her performances. Because her trunk didn't arrive in time, Vincent explained to her family, Mrs. Hooker "dressed me up in something of hers, a gown with a train and hanging about six inches on the floor all around, made out of three rainbow colored scarfs."

Vincent was enthralled with herself. "Family, I *must* have long dresses, trailing ones . . . very graceful & floaty." From then on, audiences and critics would exclaim over the dramatic, flowing gowns in which Vincent performed her readings.

Money concerns were always on her mind. The theatrical life was not taking off the way she or her supporters had expected. She was getting auditions, but she had yet to win a role. She decided to accept a position she had initially declined as "social secretary" to Mrs. Thompson, one of the benefactors who had funded her Vassar education.

Mrs. Thompson had made it clear this was a job in name only; what she wanted was to give Vincent the opportunity to write poetry, to be taken care of, and to earn a salary. Tempting as it was, it wasn't the free lifestyle Vincent envisioned. Yet as the autumn drew on, her financial worries gave the offer new appeal. By October 27 she was writing to Cora and Norma about the luxurious life she was leading on the Thompsons' country estate.

"It is eleven o'clock in the morning. I am still in bed," she began. Every morning at nine o'clock a maid brought her an elegant breakfast tray, complete with embroidered napkin and flowers, and propped her up among the pillows, pinning back her hair and helping her into her negligee. For a girl from Camden, Maine, even one who had been to Vassar and lived in New York City, it was like a fairy tale. She stayed for three weeks before the city's allure pulled her back.

Living again at the YWCA on East 52nd Street, Vincent tried to keep track of her expenses, but what was in the accounting book Caroline Dow gave her and what was in her pocketbook was never the same. She made up an extra column called "Lost in the Shuffle." In early November she had $55.05. That was the last entry she made.

At the back of the accounting book, however, she made a different list, one she did keep. It was a list of the poems she was sending out to magazines—and it was long—but by the end of 1917, she had sold only one poem, a sonnet that began "Time does not bring relief," to the *Century*.

She continued to woo Norma to New York. She clipped "help wanted" ads from newspapers and sent them to her. When Norma finally agreed to move, Vincent was thrilled at the prospect of living with her sister again. "I'm as crazy to see you as if I were going to be married to you—no one is such good pals as we are."

They found a good-sized room with a double bed and a stove for heat on West 9th Street, in the heart of

Greenwich Village, the downtown neighborhood filled with artistic, intellectual, and political energy. The Village was home to freethinkers, eccentrics, and artists of every kind, who gathered to drink, dance, and argue in bars and restaurants and at all-night parties. Rents and food were cheap. A left-wing newspaper called the *Masses* reflected the intellectual and political aura of the neighborhood. Socialism, anarchism, and nontraditional ideas about love and relationships flourished. It was the perfect place for free-spirited Vincent.

Kathleen was now at Vassar, and on December 2 the three sisters had a joyous meeting at Grand Central Terminal, amazed to be breakfasting together in the big city. Only Cora was missing—although she would soon be closer. She had given up nursing and was going to live with relatives in Bridgeport, Connecticut, weaving hairpieces again. Vincent was determined to bring her to New York as soon as she could.

A bitterly cold winter began that December—so cold that the sisters once stayed in bed together for two days to keep warm. Soon after Norma's arrival, Vincent finally found a theater that wanted her. She auditioned for a role with the Provincetown Players, a theater group that had started on Cape Cod in the summer of 1915 and moved to MacDougal Street in the Village in the fall of 1916. Its purpose was to encourage the writing of new American plays. One of the best-known playwrights of the 20th century, Eugene O'Neill, got his start with the group. Lesser known today is the writer Floyd Dell, who was also associate editor of the *Masses*. It was Floyd's play, *The Angel Interludes*, for which Vincent auditioned.

Floyd remembered in his autobiography, "A slender little girl with red-gold hair came to the greenroom over the theatre and read Annabelle's lines. She looked her frivolous part to perfection and read the lines so winningly that she was at once engaged—at a salary of nothing at all, that being our artistic custom."

Both Vincent, second from right, and Norma, fourth from left, were often seen onstage during their early years in Greenwich Village. *Peter A. Juley & Son, Library of Congress Prints and Photographic Division, Washington, DC*

Vincent quickly won Floyd's heart. He wrote, "I fell in love with her voice at once; and with her spirit, when I came to know it, so full of indomitable courage." Vincent welcomed and returned his attention and affection, but she had no intention of settling down with anyone.

Undeterred, Floyd found Vincent and Norma a larger, warmer, cheaper room at 139 Waverly Place, and helped them fix it up. When they were sick, he brought them toasted crumpets, roast beef and tongue sandwiches on rye bread, and made them coffee. He asked Vincent to marry him, but she refused, saying, "Never ask a girl poet to marry you, Floyd."

She continued to act in his plays, and stayed by his side during the April 1918 trial against the *Masses*, when the magazine's editors were accused of treason for their antimilitary stance. But through it all she kept her emotional distance. Deep and enduring as their friendship would be, her November 1918 poem, "Daphne," expresses her warning to Floyd—and perhaps to future lovers, as well.

> *Why do you follow me?—*
> *Any moment I can be*
> *Nothing but a laurel tree.*
>
> *Any moment of the chase*
> *I can leave you in my place*
> *A pink bough for your embrace.*

> *Yet if over hill and hollow*
> *Still it is your will to follow*
> *I am off; —to heel, Apollo!*

Soon after Vincent won the part of Annabelle, *Renascence and Other Poems* was published, in December 1917, to high acclaim. Edward J. Wheeler, one of the *Lyric Year* judges who had voted against giving a cash prize to "Renascence," wrote her a letter that was especially meaningful. He gushed, "I had not known that there was so much beauty in the world. . . . I don't know how you could do it,—you, a mere school-girl. I can't say anything, as yet, of critical value. I don't want to. I am just feasting."

Cold as the winter was, Vincent was flush with the warmth of success. Not only had her book been successfully received, she was asked to officially join the Provincetown Players after Floyd's play opened. Norma had some work as a seamstress, and soon began to act with the troupe, too. Poor but joyously swept up in their creative and social lives, they neglected their correspondence to Cora, who heard from Kathleen and other relatives about the poverty they were living in.

In January she wrote, full of worry and admonishment: "Oh girls, your mother has been in hell! . . . So far away from any knowledge of how you are faring . . . or what you are going to do, as if I were on some other planet."

Norma responded, assuring their mother that although they were both a little sick at the moment, they had many dear friends, such as Floyd ("like a wonderful brother to me and a bit more than a brother to Vincent"), to care for them and that she shouldn't worry. Vincent added that she had written "some quite good poems lately."

She sold five of those poems to *Poetry* magazine, which published them in the June 1918 issue. They were light, flippant verses and epitomized the bohemian spirit and life of Greenwich Village. "First Fig" became Vincent's best-known poem.

My candle burns at both ends;
It will not last the night;
But ah, my foes, and oh, my friends—
It gives a lovely light!

Another, "Thursday," expresses her cavalier attitude toward love.

And if I loved you Wednesday,
Well, what is that to you?
I do not love you Thursday—
So much is true.

And why you come complaining
Is more than I can see.
I loved you Wednesday,—yes—but what
Is that to me?

Yet another, "The Penitent," ends with a sassy admittance of bad behavior.

> *"I've been a wicked girl," said I;*
> *"But if I can't be sorry, why,*
> *I might as well be glad!"*

These poems established Vincent's reputation as the "It Girl" of Greenwich Village. She was becoming the symbol of the modern woman, one who could think, love, and live as freely as she chose.

In February 1918 poet Arthur Davison Ficke, with whom she'd led a warm correspondence since the publication of "Renascence" in *The Lyric Year* in 1912, stopped in New York. Now an army major, Arthur was on his way to France, and he wanted to meet Vincent at last. As it turned out, he and Floyd Dell were good friends. Floyd brought Arthur to the apartment on Waverly Place to have dinner with Vincent, Norma, and Norma's beau, the painter and actor Charles Ellis, whom she had met through the Provincetown Players.

Sitting on the floor and joking, they ate sandwiches and pickles Charles had bought at a nearby delicatessen. In spite of Floyd's presence, Arthur and Vincent immediately fell in love. He had only a few days in New York, and he and Vincent spent most of that time together.

She wrote to Kathleen: "He's exceedingly handsome, tall and curly-headed and with a lovely voice and—oh my God, *everything*! He's gone to France!—I am crazy about him, and he's gone, he's gone." Not only gone, Arthur was also married. While he and Vincent exchanged deeply felt love letters for several years, they went forward to become lifelong friends.

In June 1918 Cora finally arrived in New York. Expecting her, the sisters had moved to larger quarters at 25 Charlton Street. Cora, now 55, took quickly to life in the Village. "Mrs. Millay cut her hair short like the rest of the girls, wrote poetry, sewed costumes for the Provincetown Players and acted in one of the plays," remembered Floyd. One of Vincent's suitors wrote later that Cora was "most extraordinary. . . . She sometimes made remarks that were startling from the lips of a little old lady."

The family was almost complete, save for Kathleen, who was struggling at Vassar. She found the studies difficult and felt left out of her family. She wrote often, complaining about feeling isolated and doing "rotten work."

Money was always hard to come by. So when Vincent received an invitation from W. Adolphe Roberts, the new editor of *Ainslee's* magazine, she went to the meeting eagerly. Mr. Roberts was immediately charmed by Vincent and offered her 50 cents a line for her poetry. She agreed, giving him "Daphne." He became yet another admirer of Vincent's, taking her to dinner often, when they would talk about poetry and love. In his memoir he described "the light from her sea-green eyes seeming to make the freckles across her nose like a tiger lily's spots, her mouth elfin," and noted that "without setting to do so she created a cult. . . . The girls of the 1920s applied to themselves not only the gay flippancies of *A Few Figs from Thistles* [Vincent's second volume of poetry], but the mighty pulsations to be found in her sonnets."

Realizing she could never make enough money publishing her poems in magazines, Vincent mentioned the possibility of writing fiction, and Mr. Roberts encouraged her. She chose the pseudonym Nancy Boyd, her great-grandmother's maiden name. Starting in May 1919, issues of *Ainslee's* often ran stories by Nancy Boyd—Vincent and Mr. Roberts called them "potboilers" (writings produced quickly, solely to make money, and usually without much literary merit)—and poems by Edna St. Vincent Millay, sometimes on the same page.

By then Cora and the three sisters—Kathleen having left Vassar—were living on West 19th Street, between 9th and 10th Avenues, where they had moved in February. The rent was $21 a month. Thanks to the stories *Ainslee's* was buying for $75 each (plus a novella for $400), Vincent was finally able to keep up with family expenses.

Without having to worry as much about money, Vincent found poems pouring forth. From that summer into the summer of 1920 she wrote many of her most famous sonnets, mostly about love, with lines like: "What lips my lips have kissed, and where, and why / I have forgotten"; "Pity me that the heart is slow to learn / What the swift mind beholds at every turn"; "Need we say it was not love / now that love is perished?" The poems she wrote during this prolific period were collected into what should have been her second book, *Second April*, but Mitchell Kennerley delayed its production, and *A Few Figs from Thistles* appeared first, in the spring of 1920. Published by bookseller Frank Shay, it immediately became a bestseller in the Village. The volume includes the melodic, and now very well-known, poem entitled "Recuerdo," which describes a romantic night out with Nicaraguan poet Salomòn de la Selva, yet another admirer of Vincent's.

All of the Millays were now involved in the Provincetown Players. Cora even sang in a production of Eugene O'Neill's *The Moon of the Caribbees*. Vincent was not only acting, she was writing her own plays, which were produced to fine reviews. When her antiwar allegory *Aria da Capo* opened in December 1919, it was praised in the *New York Times* as "the most beautiful and the most interesting play in the English language now to be seen in New York."

In February 1920 Vincent traveled to Cincinnati to present a lecture and poetry reading to the Ohio Valley Poetry Society. The city received her on her 28th birthday, and Vincent felt in top form. "I have never made such a thorough success of anything as I made of my lecture here," she wrote her family.

A few months later, at a cocktail party in the Village, she met two young editors of *Vanity Fair* magazine, John Peale Bishop and Edmund "Bunny" Wilson. Close friends, the two had long been aware of Vincent's work and were eager to meet her.

Vincent arrived straight from a performance at the Provincetown Playhouse. She was persuaded to recite some of her poems, and Bunny remembered in a memoir that "the company hushed and listened as people do to music." He and John immediately fell for Vincent, who playfully encouraged them both. Bunny wrote that falling in love with her was "almost inevitable a consequence of knowing her in those days," describing her "intoxicating effect on people . . . the spell that she exercised on many, of all ages and both sexes."

Bunny and John brought her work to *Vanity Fair*, which was a high step above *Ainslee's* in reputation—and paid considerably better. The editor, Frank Crowninshield, soon began to pay her a regular allowance for her poems and the prose by Nancy Boyd. W. Adolphe Roberts understood that this was a much better opportunity for Vincent, and gracefully gave up his role as her magazine publisher.

In the summer of 1920 Vincent rented a cottage in Truro, on Cape Cod, for her family. They reveled in being by the sea again; the cottage was little more than a shack, but it was set back from the dunes of Longnook Beach in a pine hollow. Wild roses grew out front and there was a swing on the porch. Vincent entertained both John and Bunny there, separately, and during one visit, she received a marriage proposal from Bunny. She promised to think about it, but Bunny soon realized she would never say yes.

Later that summer, Vincent decided that she needed to live on her own in New York. In the autumn she moved into a room at 77 West 12th Street. John and Bunny continued to pursue her, and Frank Crowninshield complained "that it was difficult to have both his assistants in love with one of his most brilliant contributors."

Vincent had indeed become one of *Vanity Fair*'s shining stars, and she relished her newfound celebrity status. "I am becoming very famous," she gloated in a letter to Hal Bynner. "The current Vanity Fair has a whole page of my poems, and a photograph of me. . . . Besides I just got a prize of a hundred dollars in Poetry, for the Beanstalk."

Although she was still anxiously awaiting the publication of *Second April*, by the end of 1920 she had published 77 poems, eight prose pieces, and two books of poetry. Her play *Aria da Capo* had been such a huge success that a publisher was negotiating for the rights. But she was ready for something new, writing to Cora that New York was getting too crowded and busy for her to work.

An opportunity came from Mr. Crowninshield; he suggested Vincent become a foreign correspondent for *Vanity Fair*. She would live in Europe and produce two pieces a month, one by Nancy Boyd and one by Edna St. Vincent Millay.

On December 17 Vincent and Norma attended Kathleen's wedding to playwright Howard Young at the Brevoort Hotel in New York. On January 4, 1921, Vincent sailed for Paris.

We were very tired, we were very merry—
We had gone back and forth all night on the ferry.
It was bare and bright, and smelled like a stable—
But we looked into a fire, we leaned across a table,
We lay on a hill-top under the moon;
And the whistles kept blowing, and the dawn came soon.

We were very tired, we were very merry—
We had gone back and forth all night on the ferry;
And you ate an apple, and I ate a pear,
From a dozen of each we had bought somewhere;
And the sky went wan, and the wind came cold,
And the sun rose dripping, a bucketful of gold.

We were very tired, we were very merry—
We had gone back and forth all night on the ferry.
We hailed, "Good morrow, mother!"
to a shawl-covered head,
And bought a morning paper, which neither of us read;
And she wept, "God bless you!" for the apples and pears,
And we gave her all our money but our subway fares.

—*"Recuerdo," from* A Few Figs from Thistles, *1920*

European Adventures

1921–1923

"I was awake long before dawn this morning," Vincent wrote Cora from onboard the *Rochambeau*, "couldn't sleep for excitement." After the monotony of seeing nothing but ocean for eight days, this gray and rainy morning they had finally reached the English Channel. Vincent was eager for her first glimpse of France.

Settling into the comfortable Hôtel des Saints Pères in the Latin Quarter on the Left Bank (Paris's equivalent of Greenwich Village), she was immediately drawn into the city's social and cultural life, attending parties, plays, and concerts. She was a lively presence at cafés where fellow expatriate writers, musicians, and artists gathered.

Wearing a fashionable evening gown, Vincent danced to jazz bands with men and with women, provoking jealousy among their partners. She wrote in the mornings and walked the city—"miles and miles," she wrote Norma—in the afternoons. She devoted her work to the flippant sketches for *Vanity Fair* that provided her with income she badly needed and, soon, to a play that Vassar commissioned from her for the college's 60th anniversary.

In spite of the gaiety of Paris, and a new beau (an Englishman, but unfortunately, a married one with three children), Vincent was often homesick. In June, now living at the Hôtel de l'Intendance on rue de l'Université (still in the Latin Quarter), she complained in a letter to Cora: "I have been really homesick for the last few days. It has been ages since I heard from any of you, and besides that they are putting my play on at Vassar just about now, and I am crazy to see it."

Emotional, she went on: "Mother do you know, almost all people love their mothers, but I have never met anybody in my life, I think, who loved his mother as much as I love you. . . . You brought me up in the tradition of poetry, and everything I did you encouraged." She enclosed a small pink flower.

She missed her sisters, too. "Dearest Darling Baby Sister 'Lovèd Hunk," she wrote Norma, "I have your beautiful photograph right up in front of me on my work table, & as I do a lot of work, I just naturally has to look at it, whether I want to or not, but the joke is on it, because I allus wants to."

The play for Vassar, *The Lamp and the Bell*, starred Kathleen. Kathleen's husband, Howard, wrote to Vincent in early July about its success and included an admiring clipping from the *New-York Tribune*. Originally entitled *Snow White & Rose Red* and written in verse, the play focused on the love between two young women who eventually become stepsisters. It was performed on the campus green where Vincent herself had often shone.

Late in July she decided to go to what she called "the seashore"—actually Dieppe on the English Channel, the nearest beach to Paris—with a group of painters and writers. She was thrilled at the prospect of being by the sea again, she wrote Cora. In that letter she invited her mother to join her abroad. It would take longer than either Vincent or Cora wanted, but by spring the two would be together in Europe.

With that letter, Vincent also enclosed a new poem—the only one she'd written since leaving the United States. She called it "The Ballad of the Harp-Weaver" and dedicated it to her mother. She had purposefully stayed away from writing poetry recently, feeling that she was writing almost from habit, and hoping that when she returned to it her poems would be fresh and "possibly in a newer form."

This new one was decidedly different from all her others. Very long, written in the four-line rhythmic verse style of an old-fashioned ballad, and incorporating repetition, the poem is narrated by a young boy who lives with his mother in poverty as great as their love.

One Christmas Eve, the boy wakes at night to see his mother miraculously weaving bright gold threads into a wardrobe "of a king's son / Just my size," even as she freezes to death in the process.

Published in *Vanity Fair* in the June 1922 issue, a year after she wrote it, the poem met with mixed reactions. Bunny Wilson told her it belonged in a woman's magazine, given its leaning toward the sentimental. But her mother and sisters loved it, finding in it resonances of their early poverty in Maine, the bonds between them, the sacrifices Cora had made for her girls, and her passion for the arts, which she had passed on to them.

Vincent stayed in Dieppe into September and then endured a rough crossing of the Channel to spend a few weeks with a friend in the English countryside, where she enjoyed her first taste of tea with milk. Mitchell Kennerley had finally brought out *Second April*, which was received with excellent reviews. *Atlantic Monthly* noted, among other things, "She never clutters her pages with the second-hand, or with the merely ornamental, or with the merely smart," and the magazine singled out a sonnet Vincent had written for Arthur Davison Ficke after their romantic three days in New York in 1918: "Into the golden vessel of great song / Let us pour all our passion."

From England, Vincent traveled to Rome. Her married Englishman had given her up, and she had met another man in Paris, John Carter, who was now waiting for her in Rome. He was connected to the American ambassador to Italy, knew the country well, and promised they would show her a wonderful time.

Soon after her arrival, the ambassador suggested an adventure to the two young people. After a rocky history during and after World War I, the country of Albania had just had its borders officially recognized and was now open to Western travelers. John and Vincent decided to follow the ambassador's recommendation to explore this little-known country.

They spent nearly four weeks in the beautiful, rugged land. The first day they rode 10 hours on horseback through the mountains. It was only Vincent's second time on horseback in her life. Just three days later she was back in the saddle for a 12-hour journey from Elbasan to Cavaja. She fell in love with the little lavender flowers—lulets, she learned to call them—that grew by the roadsides, flowers unlike any she'd ever seen. She brought some back with her and sent a few to Cora.

Everywhere she went in Europe, in fact, she discovered new flowers and herbs and reveled in the foreign names for familiar ones. In front of the Tuileries Gardens in Paris were long rows of what she knew as field daisies, but the French cultivated them and called them *marguerites*. In Dieppe she saw yarrow and Queen Anne's lace, which she was informed was wild parsley, and learned the names of 54 wildflowers she had never known—hound's-tongue, fleabane, lady's bedstraw—except for occasional encounters in poetry. She was amazed at the thousands of red poppies that grew wild in wheat fields throughout the countryside.

In Albania she and John Carter tore apart ripe pomegranates, eating the seeds and letting the fruit's red juice stain their faces; they drank Turkish coffee and listened to the muezzin (a Muslim crier) calling the townspeople to prayer before daybreak. In spite of getting fleas, and "in spite of all the hardships and inconveniences of traveling in a country with no railroads or public conveyances of any kind, as a matter of fact for the most part no roads at all except a bridle path through the mountains," Vincent declared the trip to be the most thrilling one of her life.

While Vincent was on her European adventures, she received exciting news from Norma. She and Charles Ellis had married, and moved into an apartment over the Washington Square Book Store on West 8th Street. Norma warned Vincent, whose 30th birthday was quickly approaching, about two things: first, not to make any rash decisions in her life just because both her younger sisters were married now; and, second, "If you should ever write me curb your desire to write me as Mrs. Charles Ellis please as I am still and shall be Norma Millay. God pity you if you Mrs. Me. You'll suffer!" Norma was making a name as an actress and was not about to let that name disappear from the theater world.

Vincent was back in Rome when she received Norma's announcement. Soon she was traveling again, to Vienna and then Budapest. She wanted badly to bring Cora to

Europe, as promised, but was continually struggling to get by on the income from her stories for *Vanity Fair.*

In Vienna Vincent received a bewildering letter from Arthur Davison Ficke. He revealed that Hal Bynner told him he had asked Vincent to marry him. Arthur supported the idea. "For many years I have wanted to do it myself. But since I can't, I think it would be awfully nice if you two got married and then adopted me."

To her even greater surprise, Hal added his own note at the bottom of the letter. "What about that? I am beginning to think there is no such go-between as the Atlantic Ocean. Why have you never answered? Is there no answer?"

She had never received Hal's letter with the proposal. But this was at least the third proposal she had received in her life, and from a man she had adored, a dear friend, a man "bound in the memories of my childhood," as she wrote him. She decided to accept. "Do you really want me to marry you?—Because if you really want me to, I will. I have thought for a long time that someday I should marry you."

When she heard nothing back, she sent a cable: "YES HAL." When silence followed, she sent another, a week later. This one said only: "YES."

Hal finally wrote back, rethinking his proposal. The three of them corresponded about the idea for months. Vincent assured Hal that even though she loved Arthur, she loved him, too. And it wasn't just that Arthur was married and not free. Arthur, she wrote, "is something to me that nobody else is. But why should that trouble you, Hal? Don't you love several people?"

It was Arthur who eventually realized how deeply his and Hal's friendship was suffering through this experience. He believed it would be destroyed if Hal and Vincent married. He convinced Hal the marriage would not be a good idea, and Hal promptly wrote Vincent.

All the drama had driven Vincent to postpone Cora's planned trip. Now, having received a $500 advance for a novel, Vincent sent $400 of it to her mother and cabled her: "PREPARE SAIL ROCHAMBEAU SOON POSSIBLE." On March 28 Cora boarded the *Rochambeau* in New York. Vincent would meet the boat in Le Havre. It was the same journey she herself had taken, on the same boat, 14 months earlier.

In Paris Cora went along with the dancing and drinking at clubs, cabarets, and cafés, falling into Parisian bohemian life as easily as she had taken to her daughters' reckless lifestyle in Greenwich Village. Vincent assured Norma that everybody was crazy about their mother and that Cora was enjoying every minute. They socialized with well-known writers and artists of the day, like the poet Hilda Doolittle, who called herself H.D., and the painter Man Ray, who eventually painted Vincent's portrait.

Vincent and Cora took side-by-side rooms in the Hôtel Venetia, next door to the Café de la Rotonde, where they drank coffee or cocktails and had most of their meals— usually *choucroute garnie* ("fried sauerkraut trimmed with boiled potatoes, a large slice of ham & a fat hot dog, yum, yum, werry excillint," Vincent described to Norma). Sometimes they bought fruit, dates, crackers, and cheeses and ate in one of their rooms.

After five weeks in Paris, Cora had seen more of the city than Vincent had in her first five months, visiting churches, museums, and tourist sites like the Eiffel Tower and the famous Père Lachaise Cemetery. She exulted in viewing paintings by Paul Gauguin, James Abbott McNeill Whistler, Paul Cézanne, Claude Monet, and Édouard Manet. She attended recitals, ballet, and the theater. In June Arthur came to Paris, too (bringing with him a new young woman, Gladys Brown, a painter), and threw Cora a luncheon party.

Cora was living the high life with her daughter. But one thing troubled her: Vincent was obviously sick. She had suffered from stomach problems her entire life, but in Europe she grew worse than ever and was ill much of the time. Cora blamed the French cuisine—and the madcap lifestyle. (Today Vincent's illness would be diagnosed as Crohn's disease—chronic inflammation of the gastrointestinal tract.) She determined they should go to England.

They traveled to London in early July with Arthur and Gladys. By mid-July Cora and Vincent were in the village of Shillingstone in Dorset, sharing a four-room thatched hut in the countryside with the couple who owned it. Friends from Paris, Dwight Townsend and Tess Root, followed and found lodgings in the village, too. Before long, Gladys arrived as well, Arthur having returned to the United States. Gladys wanted to paint the Shillingstone Hills, and they found her a room nearby. The villagers were often surprised to find her painting in the road.

Vincent also took over a tiny one-room hut with straw flooring in a neighboring field, where she wrote. Every day Cora brought her a basket lunch of food she had prepared: meat, baked potatoes, salad, bread pudding with cream, and fresh milk to drink. They went for daily long walks, listening to the larks and bluebirds, picking poppies, honeysuckle, and other flowers.

Under Cora's care, Vincent began to improve. By September she felt well enough to make a short trip to London with Tess Root to meet with an English publisher about bringing out a volume of her poems.

She wasn't making any progress, however, on the novel she had promised publisher Horace Liveright—and for which she had received the $500 advance more than six months earlier. In November she tried to convince Mr. Liveright that it was almost done and that it was "working itself out beautifully." She titled it *Hardigut*, alluding to her chronic stomach problems, and explained that her characters' attitudes about food were meant to be an allegory about romantic and sexual freedom, which she strongly believed in. She promised him it would be ready for April publication.

To Norma and Charles, though, she confessed that she had barely started the novel. She also told them about a mystery story she had sent to her agent. Set in Paris, it was called "The Murder in the Fishing Cat." It took place in a restaurant named Le Chat qui Peche (the Fishing Cat), which she thought a good title. The only mystery she ever wrote, it was published under her own name in the March 1923 issue of *Century* magazine. She never finished *Hardigut*.

Cora and Vincent stayed in the country until winter, when the cold weather came. By then Vincent was ill again. To her dear Vassar friend Isobel Simpson she confided, "I have been quite respectably, but unromantically ill,—trouble arising from an improper diet, unfamiliar queer foods in Hungary and Albania, etc., which have played the devil with me."

They needed to go somewhere warm, and in December they headed for the South of France, to the town of Cassis on the Mediterranean Sea. Their plan was to continue east along the coast to Italy and then explore that country, returning to New York by June.

After a difficult trip, they arrived in Cassis, where they gathered mushroom and acorns, picked heather, wild thyme, and rosemary, and Vincent swam in the Mediterranean. But soon even the South of France grew cold, and Vincent was no better—she was weaker, in fact. It was especially bad timing that Arthur had just divorced his wife and was planning to marry Gladys. Even though she wrote him that it was "marvelous," Vincent couldn't help adding, "I shall love you till the day I die."

It was clearly time to go home. Vincent and Cora returned to Paris, and on January 17, 1923, they set sail on the SS *Rotterdam*. Vincent spent much of the voyage in bed, occasionally venturing out for tea but returning to bed before dinner, while Cora walked a mile a day, eight loops around the deck, talked with the other passengers, and wrote in her diary.

When they docked in Hoboken, New Jersey, on January 26, Vincent was so weak and tired she could not write at all. But her literary reputation was strong. *Second April*, which had been published to such acclaim in August 1921, had been reprinted twice and had sold nearly 5,000 copies, more than *Renascence*. In December Frank Shay (the bookseller in Greenwich Village who had first published *A Few Figs from Thistles*) had brought out a stapled, 20-page edition of *The Ballad of the Harp-Weaver*, with an orange cover featuring a woodcut of a mother and child. And greater literary triumphs were yet to come.

An Embarrassment
of Riches

1923–1927

Back in New York, Vincent rented rooms on Waverly Place, in the same building where her friend Tess Root lived. Cora, unable to convince Vincent to seek medical help, finally went north to Maine while Vincent, listless at best, turned 31 and tried to work on *Hardigut*.

Stomach troubles continued to plague her, depleting her energy. Friends attempted to revive her. Bunny Wilson introduced her to poet Elinor Wylie, whose first book Vincent had glowingly reviewed a few months earlier, and the two immediately became close friends. That was one of the only bright spots in her life that winter.

In the spring Tess persuaded Vincent to attend a weekend party with her in Croton-on-Hudson, one hour north of Manhattan. The town's proximity to the city, and its lovely views of the Hudson River, drew many literary Greenwich Villagers, who rented several of the houses on Mount Airy Road. That weekend's party included Arthur Davison Ficke and Gladys Brown, and Vincent's old friend Floyd Dell. Vincent was still not well, but she got her spirits up enough to take part in a game of charades one evening.

She was paired with a charming Dutch businessman, Eugen Boissevain (pronounced "bwa-se-vain"), a friend of the writer Max Eastman, with whom he was sharing a house on Mount Airy Road. She had met Max and Eugen years earlier, in the Village, and hadn't given either one of them a second thought—nor they her.

But that spring evening, surrounded by friends, Vincent and Eugen's meeting was life changing. They were assigned to play two lovers in a farce. Floyd Dell never forgot what he witnessed. "They acted their parts wonderfully—so remarkably, indeed, that it was apparent to us all that it wasn't just acting. We were having the unusual privilege of seeing a man and a girl fall in love with each other violently and in public, and telling each other so, and doing it very beautifully!"

The next day Eugen picked Vincent up in his car—a beautiful big Mercer—and drove her to his and Max's house. Quickly realizing that Vincent was not just tired but seriously ill, he called a doctor. Eugen tended devotedly to her for the following months, driving her to internists and surgeons in New York City and staying by her side through the many examinations and X-rays they performed.

While living in Eugen's Croton house and suffering from her bad health, Vincent received stunning news. A letter from Columbia University informed her that she had been nominated for the 1923 Pulitzer Prize for Poetry. When the list of winners was made public on May 14, Edna St. Vincent Millay became the first woman to win the Pulitzer Prize for Poetry. There was no greater honor she could have received. And the $1,000 prize money was just as important to her.

With this great accomplishment and filled with Eugen's love, Vincent felt ready to settle down. She wrote her mother on May 30: "Darling, do you remember meeting Eugen Boissevain one day in Waverly Place?—you will like him very much when you know him, which will be soon. And it is important that you should like him,—because I love him very much, & am going to marry him."

Who was the man who finally won the elusive poet's heart? Eugen Boissevain was one of 11 children born to an Irish mother in a wealthy, distinguished Dutch family. His paternal ancestors had made their money as shipowners, and his father had been the editor of an important Dutch newspaper. Eugen himself had built a good business importing coffee beans from Java.

Eugen was adventurous, energetic, and romantic, a lover of literature and the arts. Most important, he was a confident man who was drawn to free-spirited women.

His first wife had been the women's suffrage leader Inez Milholland, also a Vassar graduate. Coincidentally, Milholland had visited Vassar while Vincent was a student, and had made a strong impression on her. Vincent had written to Norma, "Inez Milholland (the great Suffragette of America) a Vassar grad, was back here and played a little skit for the college, a little play. She's wonderful."

Eugen, a strong believer in his first wife's feminist and political views, accompanied and cared for her on her many national lecture tours, where her fiery speeches aroused audiences. After one particularly passionate presentation in 1916, Milholland collapsed onstage. She was diagnosed with pernicious anemia, a rare blood disorder, and died in Eugen's arms several hours later. Even though she told him, as she was dying, "You go ahead and live another life," he could not think of marrying again—until that April evening in Croton-on-Hudson in 1923.

Eugen (Vincent affectionately called him "Ugin") was 12 years older than Vincent. Strong, muscular, tall, and trim, he had a charming accent and a booming laugh. His nurturing disposition and ability to run a household, cook, entertain, and garden were endearing complements to his dynamic personality. He was the right man at the right time in Vincent's life.

Vincent needed all the care Eugen could give her. The doctors allowed her to work only one hour a day and instructed her to lie down 15 hours out of every 24. She complied, yet at a July 17 consultation, her doctors were still puzzled and made the decision to perform exploratory surgery the next day. Vincent and Eugen made their own decision; they would marry in the morning.

The July 18, 1923, wedding took place on a friend's lawn in Croton. Surrounded by Norma and Charles, Arthur and Gladys, Floyd, and Eugen's brother Jan, Vincent and Eugen made their vows before the justice of the peace. Vincent wore a green-and-gold silk dress and carried an armful of roses and lilies of the valley, with a

Vincent and Eugen's wedding on July 18, 1923, was attended by Norma (holding Vincent's train), Gladys Brown, Arthur Davison Ficke (behind Gladys), Norma's husband, Charles Ellis, and Eugen's brother Jan, as well as Floyd Dell, who took this photo. *Edna St. Vincent Millay Papers, Manuscript Division, Library of Congress, Washington, DC*

red rose tucked behind one ear. Her long white veil was mosquito netting that maid of honor Norma gathered up from the porch at the last minute and draped around her head, holding the end of it with as much dignity as though it were a traditional train. After a quick brunch, dogged by reporters, the newlyweds left for New York Hospital on West 16th Street.

The surgeons made a seven-inch horizontal incision and discovered Vincent's lower intestines were, as she later wrote Kathleen, "tied down by membranes, which could not be removed." They rebuilt her intestinal tract, promising that the scar would heal and in time would scarcely be visible.

Vincent's successful surgery and her marriage made headlines in several New York newspapers: MISS MILLAY UNDER KNIFE, POETESS BRIDE TO GO UNDER KNIFE, HONEYMOONING ALONE IN HOSPITAL. Three of the papers made it front-page news.

She recovered slowly, first in Croton and then back in Greenwich Village. Arthur helped her correct the proofs for *The Harp-Weaver and Other Poems*, and Eugen handled her personal and business correspondence. He wrote Norma in the late summer that Vincent "sleeps like a guinea pig, eats like a trooper. The doctor is tickled to death."

Eugen found a tiny three-story brick house for them in the Village, at 75½ Bedford Street, known as the skinniest house in New York City. Built in 1873, it was only nine-and-a-half feet wide on the interior. The rent was

$200 a month, an amount Vincent could never have afforded on her own. Eugen's wealth, while considerably less than it had been in earlier years, should have allowed Vincent to finally stop worrying about money.

In the autumn of 1923 Eugen (seated in background) and Vincent rented the narrow little house at 75½ Bedford Street in Greenwich Village. *Jessie Tarbox Beals, Library of Congress Prints and Photographs Division, Washington, DC*

With some of her Pulitzer Prize money, she happily repaid all her family's debts in Camden, even though she fretted to Cora, "Of course, it has made quite a hole in my bank account, which I must get busy now and fill."

When Vincent was well enough, in late October, Eugen treated her to a luxurious weekend at the Ritz-Carlton Montreal. As they'd never had a honeymoon, this might have been considered one, except that he invited Norma and Kathleen to come along, and they did, enjoying the lavish accommodations and each other's company.

By November Vincent was able to travel alone again, and went to an event commemorating Susan B. Anthony and other founders of the National Woman's Party in Washington, DC. At the ceremony she recited one of her sonnets, which she later dedicated to Inez Milholland. It ends with a stirring cry to action—"Take up the song: forget the epitaph"—which now graces Vincent's own stone in the American Poets Corner in New York City's Cathedral of St. John the Divine.

She returned from Washington the same day *The Harp-Weaver and Other Poems* came out, November 19. As some of the poems had already been pronounced Pulitzer Prize–worthy, the public and the critics had been eagerly awaiting the volume. The attention lavished on her recent marriage and surgery only increased the excitement that accompanied the book's publication. Praise poured in from every direction and fueled anticipation for Vincent's upcoming 1924 lecture tours.

The first tour lasted six long weeks. Eugen was busy closing down his business so he could devote himself entirely to his wife and her booming career, so Vincent traveled alone, by train, to 20 cities, from Washington, DC, to Pittsburgh to Chicago to Cedar Rapids, Iowa. She gave more than 30 readings, winning over her ever-growing audiences.

The travel was grueling, and the attention—though exhilarating—was exhausting. Fans made a point of telling her how much they loved her poems, how they knew them by heart. Newspaper headlines described her as the "poet-girl" of American writing. Reporters couldn't stop exclaiming over her petite, "wistful, appealing" appearance.

She wrote to Eugen almost daily, humorously describing the train rides, the hotel rooms, the offbeat people she encountered, her fatigue. When he sent her roses, she kissed one of the petals and enclosed it in her return letter.

Vincent returned to New York for two weeks, and then set off again, this time with Eugen, for points farther west: Cheyenne, San Francisco, Minneapolis, Omaha, Milwaukee. In Minneapolis, where she gave two readings, the hall for the second reading had to be changed three times to accommodate the crowd, reported the local newspaper. Soon even attention-loving Vincent grew tired of being in the public eye. But she was happy to make a profit of $2,000.

She had not quite recovered from the exhausting tour when Eugen took her away again, this time on the long-overdue honeymoon, to the Far East. They began by traveling across the country again to San Francisco, then sailing from there on April 19 to Honolulu and then on to Japan. She wrote Norma from on board the ship, describing the throngs of Hawaiians who crowd the docks selling floral garlands to departing passengers. "It is considered bad luck not to throw a garland of flowers overboard upon the water as you leave the port,—an offering to the sea-god." She enclosed a pressed hibiscus flower with the letter.

In Japan they took long walking tours to sacred mountains, Buddhist shrines, waterfalls, and hot springs. By the time they left, they had walked 114 miles. In Peking, China (now known as Beijing), they got the flu and had to stay in bed for 10 days. When they were well again, they chartered a boat and sailed to surrounding small islands, swimming and sunning. They continued on to Singapore, Java, the Dutch East Indies, and India. Eugen bragged to Cora from Java that Vincent was "strong and husky. . . . We walk and climb a young mountain pretty nearly every day, or otherwise ride horses. She eats for dinner and lunch mountains of spinach, salade, and lovely vegetables, and twice a day plate fulls of rhubarb and three times a day buttermilk."

In India, though, they both fell ill again, Vincent with dysentery and Eugen with a tropical fever that put him in a Bombay hospital for a week. When they recovered, they returned to Europe, stopping first in Marseille in the South of France, and then in Paris. During that trip Eugen contracted a vein inflammation called phlebitis and had to be carried from ship or train into the hotels on a stretcher. They stayed in Paris for two weeks while Vincent, for a change, nursed her husband. Then they went to Holland, where she met his family. They returned to New York in time to host Arthur and Gladys's December 4 wedding in their Greenwich Village home.

In the spring of 1925 Vincent and Eugen moved from the little house at 75½ Bedford Street to an abandoned farm a couple of hours north, in the town of Austerlitz, New York. Two miles up a dirt road from the main thoroughfare, the 435 acres were surrounded by woods and mountains. Vincent described it as "one of the loveliest places in the world" in a letter to Cora soon after they moved in. It was costing a fortune to get the two-story clapboard house into livable condition, she wrote, but "we're so excited about it we are nearly daft." They named it Steepletop, after the tall pink flowers known as steeplebush or hardhack that grew throughout the fields and meadows.

Vincent was eager to live surrounded by nature again, and Eugen wanted to give her the peace and solitude required to write. He believed she should not be "dulled by routine acts," he told a magazine reporter. "She must ever remain open to fresh contact with life's intensities." He did everything that needed doing, determined to spare her from mundane tasks and problems so that she could keep her mind free for poetry. And, of

A view of the front entrance of the main house at Steepletop as it looked in 2015. *Courtesy of the Millay Society*

course, they entertained; Steepletop was soon filled with friends like Hal Bynner, Floyd Dell, and Elinor Wylie, and their spouses. Arthur and Gladys spent so much time there that they eventually bought their own farm in a nearby town, naming it Hardhack.

Vincent's fame continued to grow. In May 1925 she received an honorary doctorate of letters degree from Tufts College in Medford, Massachusetts. That same month she shared the stage at Bowdoin College in Maine with, among others, poets Carl Sandburg and Robert Frost in celebration of the college's centenary of the class of 1825.

In spite of the eminence of the other readers and speakers, it was Vincent who caught the imagination of students and press. The reporter for the *Christian Science Monitor* breathlessly described her voice as "by turn gay and grave, pompous and flippant. . . . If Miss Millay had not been a poet she could easily have been an actress."

Vincent was used to such flattery, but she was more deeply pleased by a writing commission she received that spring. A few months earlier she had vigorously defended the work of her friend, composer Deems Taylor, in a letter to the *New York World* music editor, who had run a critical review of a recent concert. Now Taylor had been commissioned to write an opera for the Metropolitan Opera, and he wanted Vincent to write the libretto (story). She was thrilled at this opportunity to combine her love of music and poetry, and to be writing a drama again.

She worked on it in her little writing cabin just uphill from the house at Steepletop, from the spring of 1925 until the last months of 1926. In the warm months balmy breezes flowed in through the windows, while the surrounding pine trees kept the cabin shaded. In the winter months she wrote by the warmth of its wood stove. Titled *The King's Henchman*, the three-act opera takes place in 10th-century England and is based on legendary and historical figures.

While Vincent worked on the libretto, she still struggled with her health. Headaches plagued her, causing dark spots in her vision. She was weak and tired, and every few days of work cost her many more in bed. The trips to doctors, the X-rays and tests began again, with no conclusive results—except the diagnosis that Vincent was now, at the very least, suffering a nervous breakdown. She was advised to rest and exercise in the good air of Steepletop.

In the fall of 1925 Cora came to help Eugen care for her, and took over much of the household work. She stayed into the spring. Eugen handled Vincent's correspondence and read to her. He maintained his good humor and optimism, teaching a local chiropractor how to use snowshoes so he could make it to Steepletop to treat Vincent three times a week. Vincent managed to finish the libretto at the end of 1926. Now able to handle some of her own correspondence, she wrote to relatives in October that her health was slowly improving and described how very exciting it was to see the first act of *The King's Henchman* bound into a book marked "Solely for use at the first performances of the Metropolitan Opera Company, New York." She reported that she and Eugen would soon travel to Santa Fe, to visit the Fickes, who were living there since Arthur had developed pulmonary tuberculosis, a kind of lung infection.

The trip west was a wonderful change from all the journeys they had been making to doctors. They camped with Gladys at the Grand Canyon, visited the Petrified Forest and the Painted Desert, and attended an American Indian dance ceremony in the town of Zuni. Then they went back east to greet 1927 and await the debut of *The King's Henchman*.

The Poet as Celebrity

1927–1937

"The greatest American opera!" proclaimed the *New Yorker* magazine after *The King's Henchman* premiered at the Metropolitan Opera House on February 17, 1927. Vincent and Deems Taylor's collaboration was successful beyond anybody's hopes. The theater was sold out, with thick crowds standing in every available space. The composer and librettist sat in a box with their spouses, while Cora, Norma, Kathleen, and the sisters' husbands watched from the orchestra.

The audience called for Deems and Vincent at the end of each act, and when the final curtain fell there were 17 curtain calls. Vincent wore a red-and-gold dress with an awkwardly long train that she kept stepping on with her red slippers. Her health troubles had brought her weight down to 96 pounds, but onstage she couldn't stop smiling.

The opera played for several more weeks and eventually embarked on a 30-city tour. Other reviews were as exuberant as the *New Yorker*'s, which had also run a profile of Vincent (albeit filled with errors) just prior to the opera's opening. Published in book form, the libretto sold out four printings in 20 days.

Back at Steepletop, Vincent was thrilled to read a front-page news story in the March 9 issue of the *World*. The piece calculated how much money she had earned in royalties from the 10,000 copies of the book that had sold so far. "That the amount of royalties I get . . . should be of front page interest to the great New York public—well, I just sat for ten minutes with my eyes sticking out, drinking it in," she wrote in the white leather-bound diary that Lawrence Tibbett, who sang the role of the King, had given her on opening night. "Oh what a thrilling winter this has been!" Adding to her joy was her weight gain; she was up to 98 pounds.

She and Eugen missed the camaraderie of being backstage at the Metropolitan Opera House, so on March 11 they traveled by horse and sleigh through heavy snow to catch the train to Manhattan for a repeat experience. On their return, again going by horse and sleigh for the last leg of the trip, the horses accidentally plunged into a thicket of bushes, and a tree branch hit Vincent in the left eye, scratching her cornea. For weeks she could neither read nor write, and her headaches grew worse.

But at least she continued to gain weight; when poet Elinor Wylie and her husband visited in early April, Vincent noted that she was now 104 pounds, thanks greatly to Eugen's continued care. He brought her and Elinor breakfast, which they enjoyed by the fireplace in Vincent's bedroom. In the evenings Vincent played Chopin, Bach, and Beethoven on the piano as Elinor sat nearby reading.

That spring Eugen and Vincent worried about wearing themselves out by doing too much farming, but they couldn't resist building a pasture fence for their cows. And when Cora arrived, all three of them did more landscaping, planting a rose garden and enjoying the wild-apple trees, yellow willows, and the song of the yellow-breasted meadowlarks. They hired more help: a new cook and a stenographer (someone who types up what people say) named Grace, who was so overweight that sharp-tongued Vincent referred to her as "The Three Graces" in her diary.

In spite of the joys of living surrounded by beautiful nature, Vincent continued to suffer from health troubles. In June Eugen took her to Mt. Sinai Hospital in Manhattan for a relatively minor operation. Afterward she suffered from tremendous nausea and pain, which the medical staff treated with morphine—a highly addictive painkiller that was prescribed much more liberally in the 1920s than it is today.

As the summer progressed, Vincent, like many Americans, was anxiously awaiting the final verdict of a court case that had been ongoing for six years. In July 1921 two Italian immigrants, a shoemaker named Nicola Sacco and a fish peddler named Bartolomeo Vanzetti, had been accused and found guilty of holding up and murdering a paymaster and guard at a shoe factory in South Braintree, Massachusetts. Evidence of their guilt was weak, and eyewitness reports of the crime differed wildly. Many people believed that their political views—both men were anarchists and draft dodgers, as well as foreigners—had unduly influenced the judge's decision and that justice was not being served. The case divided the American people, with most liberals and intellectuals fervently supporting the two men. In April 1927, after many appeals, they were sentenced to die by the electric chair.

Vincent, her heart and mind heavy, put her outrage into a poem she called "Justice Denied in Massachusetts." Criticizing the lack of opposition to the injustice and the lack of action on behalf of the accused men, the poem begins:

> *Let us abandon then our gardens and go home*
> *And sit in the sitting room*
> *Shall the larkspur blossom or the corn grow*
> *under this cloud?*

After four more verses of bitter resignation, continuing with images of darkness and evil overcoming nature, it concludes:

Let us sit here, sit still
Here in the sitting room until we die;
At the step of Death on the walk, rise and go;
Leaving to our children's children the beautiful doorway,
And this elm
And a blighted earth to till
With a broken hoe.

As the execution date neared, Vincent felt she needed to do more than write poetry. She decided to join a protest demanding the pair be freed. She marched in front of the State House in Boston with other literary figures like John Dos Passos, Dorothy Parker, and Lola Ridge. While crowds watched, they were arrested and taken to the police station.

Eugen bailed her out and took her to the governor's office, where she hoped her fame would give her some influence. The governor was "very courteous," she noted in her diary, "but gave me no hope." She tried another tactic, traveling to the town of Clinton to see Massachusetts senator David Walsh, but it was "a fool's errand," as he wasn't even there.

Returning to the hotel, she made one more effort, writing a fervent letter to the governor; perhaps her written words would have an effect that her spoken ones had not. She emphasized the doubt that still existed about Sacco and Vanzetti's guilt. She wrote of a case in Maine in which an innocent man had been hanged. Did Governor Fuller want the blood of two possibly innocent men

In August 1927 Vincent marched in front of the Massachusetts State House in Boston to protest the upcoming execution of Nicola Sacco and Bartolomeo Vanzetti. *Edna St. Vincent Millay Papers, Archives and Special Collections, Vassar College Libraries*

on his hands? "Does no faint shadow of question gnaw at your mind? . . . There is need in Massachusetts of a great man tonight. It is not yet too late for you to be that man."

After that, there was no more to do, so she sat vigil with a few others in a hotel room. A little after midnight she learned that Sacco was gone. She was devastated. "So I knew that even at that moment Vanzetti was being strapped into the chair. Agony, agony in my heart . . . this barbarous revenge, not for anything they had done, but for what they had said and what they had thought."

Vincent's writing and actions on behalf of Sacco and Vanzetti made her even more famous, especially as her later trial in Boston for disturbing the peace that day in August took place at the same time that *The King's Henchman* was touring the country. And while she never again publicly demonstrated in a political cause, "Justice Denied in Massachusetts" would later be followed by many more politically inspired poems.

Vincent's newest volume came out in September 1928. Entitled *The Buck in the Snow*, it included poems written at Steepletop, poems that evoked the natural surroundings in which they had been composed. It was Vincent's first book of poetry in five years, eagerly anticipated and enthusiastically greeted. While American reviewers were not as impressed as the public—the book sold 40,000 copies in the first three months—English critics lauded it hugely, supporting the novelist Thomas Hardy's earlier proclamation that America's greatest contributions to the world were skyscrapers and Edna St. Vincent Millay.

Once again Vincent went on the road, giving readings across the country. In Chicago she met a handsome young poet named George Dillon, who quickly became infatuated with her. He recited a few of his poems to her, and Vincent, even in Eugen's presence, seemed equally smitten.

Though she was 36 and he was 21, the two poets began a romance that lasted many years, mostly with Eugen's blessing. Early in their relationship, Vincent wrote to George that she was "devoted" to her husband and loved him deeply, but that when she thought of George "an enchanted sickness comes over me, as if I had drunk a witch's philtre [potion]." The three were often together, Eugen inviting George to Steepletop and later to Ragged Island in Casco Bay, Maine, which he and Vincent bought in 1933.

Vincent and Eugen shared an unconventional view of marriage. They believed people should be free to love whomever they chose, and that marriage should not hinder husbands and wives from that freedom. Close and loving as Vincent and Eugen were, they each wanted the other to be happy, even if it meant sharing their spouse with another person for a while. Eugen especially understood that much of his wife's poetry was inspired by her passions. And indeed, Vincent's next book of poetry, the 52-sonnet sequence *Fatal Interview*, which includes some of her finest poems, was partially based on her passionate romance with George.

Fatal Interview was the first book of Vincent's to make the bestseller list. In the first 10 weeks after publication it sold 50,000 copies. It was the heart of the Great Depression, but people had to have her latest book—especially since it was rumored to be highly personal. She was one of America's most adored celebrities, and the public was insatiably curious about her life.

By now she and Eugen relied primarily on her income from royalties and readings to support themselves and run Steepletop. They also, along with Norma and Kathleen, helped support Cora. Both Norma and Kathleen were leading successful artistic careers, Norma as an actress and singer (she had performed in an opera at the Mayfair Theatre in New York just before the premiere of *The King's Henchman*), while Kathleen's first novel had been published in 1926 and her first volume of poems in 1927. (She eventually published another novel and two more books of poetry.) Even Cora's words saw publication; in 1928 her book of verse about an imaginary little boy, *Little Otis*, was released.

In early 1931, while awaiting publication of *Fatal Interview*, Vincent received an unexpected telegram from her uncle Bert in Camden, telling her that Cora was very ill and that Vincent should come immediately. It was the evening of February 4. She and Eugen, whose mother had died just a week earlier in Holland, decided not to wait for the next day's train but to set off by car right away. They drove for 12 hours through the snowy night, saw the sun rise as they traveled along Maine's coastline, and arrived in Camden to find that Cora had died during their journey.

Norma and Charles arrived later that day. Kathleen and Howard were in Paris, so Vincent and Norma wired Howard, asking him to gently break the news to Kathleen. Communicating via telegram, Cora's three bereft daughters decided to bury her in a large clearing at Steepletop where her beloved mountain laurel trees grew.

Norma and Vincent ceremoniously cut off three locks of their mother's hair to save. Then—with their husbands, and setting out glasses for the absent Kathleen and Howard—they drank a champagne toast to Cora. The next day they put her coffin in a hearse, and the four of them followed it in Eugen and Vincent's Cadillac through Camden, past their childhood homes, heading for Steepletop. But heavy snow in West Stockbridge, Massachusetts (about 15 miles away), brought the hearse to a stop, and the body had to be transported the rest of the way in a horse-drawn sleigh.

Cora's gravesite in the clearing was heavily frozen, and it took four days to blast through the rocky ground with dynamite. Vincent and Norma, their husbands by their sides, finally buried their mother the night of February 12. She had lived for 67 years.

The loss of Cora was an enormous blow to Vincent. Her mother had been her teacher, her champion, her companion. For a long time she could hardly write about her emotions. In response to a friend's sympathy, she responded simply, "But there's nothing to say. We had a grand time. But it's a changed world. The presence of that absence is everywhere." By summer she had begun to draft a series of poems about her mother's death, six of which were finally published in 1934.

After the publication of *Fatal Interview*, the public couldn't get enough of Vincent. In December 1932 she was invited to read her poetry on the radio. Beginning on Christmas Day, listeners across the country tuned in weekly to hear her beguiling deep voice recite her verses. The program ran for eight weeks, with an

Vincent and Norma (left and center in this undated photo of the three sisters) remained close, but Kathleen (at right) grew estranged from Vincent in the last years of her life. *Edna St. Vincent Millay Papers, Manuscript Division, Library of Congress, Washington, DC*

In January 1933 celebrated photographer Carl Van Vechten took this portrait of the famous poet. *Carl Van Vechten, Library of Congress Prints and Photographs Division, Washington, DC*

overwhelmingly positive response. It was a milestone in American radio broadcasting: the first time a literary figure received as much attention as an actor, singer, or musician. It also coincided with the publication of Vincent's play *The Princess Marries the Page*, which she had originally written at Vassar in 1917.

Her next book of poetry was entitled *Wine from These Grapes*. A more grave collection than her previous books, it held no love poems or flippant verses, but was another enormous success, selling more than 35,000 copies in the first eight weeks. (It was in *Wine from These Grapes* that she published the poems she wrote to Cora.) The country was still in the Depression, but Vincent's poems seemed to be nearly as necessary to people as bread and milk.

The most well-known poems from this collection are the 18 sonnets that appear under the title "Epitaph for the Race of Man," an examination of humanity over time. While some critics were disappointed at the book's more serious tone, the poet Louise Bogan wrote in *Poetry* magazine that the book "gives evidence" that the writer "recognizes and is prepared to meet the task of becoming a mature and self-sufficing woman and artist."

Vincent had begun to work on a drama in verse, *Conversation at Midnight*, when George Dillon asked for help translating the French poet Charles Baudelaire's book *Fleurs du Mal* (*Flowers of Evil*). Help with a few phrases soon turned into a full-blown collaboration. He and Vincent worked together through the summer of 1935 at Steepletop, and by November Vincent was writing to the publisher to complain about the design of the page proofs.

In the midst of this project, her father reappeared in her life, writing to ask her for financial support. Henry had suffered a stroke, had no income, and had fallen into debt. Vincent sent him the few dollars he needed, but by December he had died. It was Eugen, not any of Henry Millay's daughters, who went to Maine to arrange for his burial.

In December Vincent and Eugen rented a small furnished house in Delray Beach, Florida, for the winter months. Hoping for warm weather, they instead got cold and rain and fog. There was nothing to do, Eugen wrote Deems Taylor, but collect shells and drink. He was mostly joking, because Vincent continued to review proofs in great detail and sent lengthy chastising letters to the publisher, while returning to work on *Conversation at Midnight*.

With the first draft complete, Eugen and Vincent started their drive back to Steepletop on May 1, making a detour to visit the Gulf islands of Captiva and Sanibel. When they arrived at the Palms Hotel on Sanibel Island, Vincent went right to the beach while Eugen checked in and arranged for their luggage to be sent up to their room.

She had been gathering shells for a few minutes when she turned around to see flames pouring from the hotel. Everything she and Eugen had brought with them was destroyed in the fire, including her manuscript. Eugen, luckily, was unharmed.

Vincent's memory was so good that she was able to rewrite the entire play, but its publication was delayed until July 1937. Far more than the loss of her manuscript, she regretted losing one of her most precious possessions: a volume of poetry by the Latin Catullus, printed in the 17th century. She wrote a friend later that it was "the only thing that touched me emotionally, the only thing I mourned for."

Later in the summer of 1936, more misfortune came Vincent and Eugen's way. While driving up the hill to Steepletop in their station wagon, they took a sharp turn. The car door flew open and Vincent was thrown out. She rolled down an embankment, injuring her right arm and suffering a large bump on her head as well as many bruises and scratches. She could neither play the piano nor use the typewriter—the two things she most wanted and needed to do.

While some of her injuries healed with time, the accident left her with a lasting nerve injury in her back that kept her in constant pain. By 1940 she had had three operations to try to correct the problem. It was yet one more affliction for Vincent's ailing body.

In April 1937 New York University invited Vincent to receive an honorary doctorate, which greatly pleased her. It would be her fifth honorary degree; others had been bestowed on her by Tufts College, Russell Sage College, the University of Wisconsin, and Colby College. Along with that invitation came one to a dinner to be given in her honor by the chancellor's wife. She accepted both. Then she learned that the male honorary doctorate recipients were being honored at a separate dinner, at the Waldorf Astoria hotel.

Vincent was deeply offended at the sexism expressed by the separate dinners. She wrote a letter to the secretary of New York University, politely replying to a list of basic questions regarding the ceremony. Then she wrote scathingly about the discrimination. "On an occasion, then, on which I shall be present solely for reasons of scholarship, I am, solely for reasons of sex, to be excluded from the company and conversation of my fellow-doctors."

She explained that if she had known in advance about this arrangement, she would have declined both the dinner invitation and the honorary degree. "I register this objection not for myself personally," she continued, "but for all women." The next day, accompanied by

Cass Canfield (the new president of Harper & Brothers), with Eugen, Norma, and Charles in the audience, she accepted her degree.

When *Conversation at Midnight* came out, its dedication read "To Arthur Davison Ficke." Vincent had made a special trip to see Arthur to request permission to dedicate the book to him. He was very moved by her desire to publicly express their long relationship, noting in his diary how deeply important they had been to each other for nearly 25 years.

The play features an all-male cast gathered after dinner in an elegant Greenwich Village home, drinking and discussing politics, culture, women, and horse racing, all in witty, intellectual verse. It also carried a strong antiwar message, in recognition of the increasingly disturbing state of affairs in Europe in the late 1930s (which would eventually lead to World War II).

The book received an extraordinary amount of attention, even for a book of Vincent's. It was featured on the front page of the *New York Times Book Review* and was an alternate selection for the Book-of-the-Month Club. The cover of *McCall's* magazine featured a pastel portrait of Vincent by one of the top commercial artists of the time, Neysa McMein. The cover line read: AMERICA'S FOREMOST WOMAN POET.

As usual, reporters flocked to interview the author. To one from the Associated Press, Vincent explained the shift in her work: "If you don't change and develop between your first book and your tenth, then you just keep on re-writing yourself."

Vincent was 45 years old. While the witty, playful, and passionate personality of her younger years was still strong, her fervor had taken on a more somber tone over the years. She took the world's troubles into her heart, which also held her personal losses—her mother, dear friends, and dear loves. Life had changed her; her poetry had changed.

The Flickering Candle

1938–1950

In 1938 Vincent was voted one of the 10 most famous women in America. That same year, *Time* magazine proclaimed Adolf Hitler Man of the Year. The Nazi leader's devastating decisions and calamitous actions preoccupied the poet's thoughts more and more. In March Germany annexed Austria. In October German forces occupied the Sudetenland—a heavily German part of Czechoslovakia—with the assent of several European nations. In November Hitler's Nazi troops led mobs into Jewish communities in Germany and Austria, destroying more than 1,000 synagogues and shops, killing dozens of Jews, and arresting 30,000 people in a night of terror that became known as *Kristallnacht* (Night of Broken Glass). Hitler allied himself with Italian dictator

Benito Mussolini, strengthening the Fascist threat in Europe.

From Steepletop, where she was judging poets' applications for Guggenheim Fellowships, planning musical evenings at the farm, and sending poems to George Dillon (now editor of *Poetry* magazine), Vincent watched the events in Europe with growing horror. Not only was her sense of justice and liberty outraged, she also worried about Eugen's family in Holland. By the time she had started on a national reading tour to promote her upcoming volume, *Huntsman, What Quarry?*, in September, she was starting to speak out publicly against the Nazis. Many of the poems that ultimately appeared in that book address the progress of the war in Europe.

Despite the horrific events occurring in Europe, over the summer Vincent and Eugen had gardened together, hiring helpers, planting Oriental poppies, dark-blue lupines, and roses. They played tennis with a seemingly endless stream of guests. Near the inground pool Eugen placed a marble statue of a plump cherub with a quiver of arrows. Harebells, columbines, and hollyhocks grew everywhere. And while Vincent remained healthy enough to tour through the autumn months, the trips took an ever-greater toll on her.

Her final reading of the tour was at Clark University in Worcester, Massachusetts, in January 1939. She performed as beautifully as ever, although she was so exhausted by the reading and the accompanying social events that she crawled into bed afterward and fell into a deep sleep. The *Worcester Telegram & Gazette* wrote that she was as "vehement, mettlesome and exciting as one of her poems." Nobody realized this was the last national reading tour she would ever make.

As the year drew on, the horrors in Europe intensified. In March Hitler took over the rest of Czechoslovakia, and Vincent's poem entitled "Czecho-Slovakia" expressed her anguish ("If there were balm in Gilead, I would go / To Gilead for your wounds, unhappy land") and her criticism ("Honour's for sale; allegiance has its price"). The poem just made it into *Huntsman, What Quarry?*, which came out in May.

And as the year drew on, Vincent's health troubles came to the forefront again. By the time Hitler invaded Poland on September 1, 1939, Eugen was taking her to New York on a weekly basis to see both an eye doctor and an osteopath. Vincent had developed curvature of the spine, and the shoulder and back pain from the 1936 car accident had worsened. Only morphine helped.

She went under the care of Dr. Connie Guion, a distinguished physician. Dr. Guion wrote Eugen specific instructions for nursing Vincent's problems—which now included effects of menopause, which Guion believed made a woman "more susceptible to pain and less stable nervously." She instructed him to give Vincent daily injections of estrogen to lessen those effects. The morphine was also administered by injection.

In the midst of Vincent's health issues, she took part in a radio broadcast entitled "The Challenge to Civilization," focusing on the challenges the American people faced regarding the war in Europe. Aired in October, the program supported the overwhelming American position on neutrality. Vincent spoke about the danger of remaining silent when it came to losing freedom of speech anywhere in the world. Then she read her poem "Underground System" from her recent volume, which described the insidious damage to American freedom that could occur if Nazi and Fascist actions were met by silence.

By December 1, Vincent's health was such that Dr. Guion admitted her to Doctors Hospital in New York, where she stayed for three weeks. By then Vincent required ever-larger amounts of morphine to keep the pain at bay. She needed so much, in fact, that Dr. Guion didn't want any of the medical staff to be aware of the amount. She personally wrote and signed all of Vincent's prescriptions.

Vincent wasn't the only Millay suffering in 1939. Kathleen was having a difficult year, too. Howard had divorced her, and she was in continual need of money, which Vincent and Eugen regularly provided. She had been working as a writer in Los Angeles but was growing increasingly unstable mentally. Her excessive drinking only contributed to her poor mental state. She returned to New York in the spring, hoping she could find work more easily there, but instead she grew more and more depressed.

In July she admitted herself to New York Hospital, where she was diagnosed with chronic alcoholism, high blood pressure, and psychoneurosis; she remained in the hospital well into August. Her psychiatrist wrote to Eugen that many of Kathleen's mental problems were rooted in an envy of Vincent's fame and a belief that Vincent had stolen some of her ideas for her own work.

Even as Kathleen's letters to them grew nasty, Eugen and Vincent continued to give her money and pay her medical bills. Soon, though, they couldn't afford to support Kathleen financially; they themselves were constantly drawing money from Vincent's publisher, Harper & Brothers, against future royalties from her books. By April 1940, with both her medical bills and Kathleen's requiring large sums, Vincent was about to go into debt to Harper. She was working on her next book, *Make Bright the Arrows*, which would not be published until November.

She wrote the poems for that book in spite of several more hospital stays in 1940. Continuing to rely on morphine and numerous other medications, as well as a tremendous amount of alcohol, she composed the antiwar verses that comprise the volume. When the book was published, she sent a copy to George Dillon with a letter that explained, "There are a few good poems, but it is mostly . . . a book of impassioned propaganda, into which a few good poems got bound up because they happened to be propaganda, too." (In 1946 she would describe these antiwar poems as "hastily written and hotheaded pieces.") Reviewers were not very kind, though the *New York Times* reviewer did note that "Miss Millay may have written more nicely, but she has never written more strongly, with absolute belief and accuracy."

At Christmas she sent a copy to her old Vassar friend Charlotte "Charlie" Babcock Sills and was distressed at the response. Charlie had three young-adult sons and was deeply hurt and angry that Vincent would send her a volume of rousing verse that might send her boys to war. Vincent wrote back at length, insisting that "what I am trying to do with every bit of my strength . . . is not to get this country into war, but to keep it out of war."

The war had, as she and Eugen feared, hit his family hard. When Holland finally fell to Germany in May 1940, the Boissevains lost all their assets. The fall of Holland was followed in June by the Nazi invasion of Paris. News reports of that invasion in the New York papers were accompanied by Vincent's impassioned poem entitled "Lines Written in Passion and in Deep Concern for England, France, and My Own Country." The poem pleaded:

> *Oh, build, assemble, transport, give,*
> *That England, France and we may live,*
> *Before tonight, before too late*
> *To those who build our country's fate*

It subsequently ran in newspapers all over the country and was hailed by many as an important poem of the new war. Harper published it in the autumn as a 10-page booklet, preceding publication of *Make Bright the Arrows*. It had a new title: "There Are No Islands Any More." Vincent took no royalties so that all proceeds could go to war-relief agencies. The paper manufacturers and the printer provided their services for free.

Throughout the writing and manufacturing of this booklet—as well as the writing of the poems that would soon appear in *Make Bright the Arrows*—Vincent continued to be quite ill. She rarely left Steepletop—rarely left her bedroom, in fact. She did manage, in January 1941, to give a public reading at Carnegie Hall, though it would be her very last one. Her 100-line poem "Invocation to the Muses" called for the muses to help a world gone mad: "How shall we heal without your help a world / By these wild horses torn asunder?"

June 10, 1942, saw one of the greatest atrocities of World War II. Nazis marched into the peaceful village of Lidice in Czechoslovakia. Claiming that the village harbored the assassins of an important Nazi, they razed every structure and killed or deported most of the village's inhabitants. The world was outraged; the president of the Writers' War Board asked Vincent to write a piece in commemoration of the village.

She produced a book-length narrative poem titled "The Murder of Lidice." Movie actor Paul Muni read it on the radio on October 19, and it was heard not only throughout North America but also in England and other European countries. Translations were broadcast to South America, as well. Harper & Brothers published it later that year. Emotionally moving, the poem describes in detail, among much else, the anguish felt by the dying, and mourns the village:

The whole world holds in its arms today
The murdered village of Lidice,
Like the murdered body of a little child.

Listener response was overwhelming, though some friends and critics continued to consider Vincent's anti-war poetry hysterical and unbecoming of her talent.

Norma was among those moved by the radio broadcast. She wrote to Vincent about how "alive" it had been, but also voiced her worries about her sister's health, and her and Eugen's isolation at Steepletop for the coming winter. Vincent wrote back warmly, but stayed put.

While Norma and Vincent remained close, Kathleen continued to harangue Vincent and Eugen, even to the point of attempting blackmail. In September 1943 she died of acute alcoholism, but at that point Vincent herself was too ill to attend the funeral.

In January 1943 Vincent received the Poetry Society of America's Frost Medal for distinguished lifetime achievement in poetry, making her the second woman and sixth person to be awarded this honor. But from 1943 to 1947 she was unable to write any poetry, except for one piece of propaganda for the Writer's War Board in May 1944. She struggled with reducing her drug dosages, sometimes succeeding, sometimes not. During those years Vincent was hospitalized five times.

By 1945 her reputation had severely deteriorated. Many of her books were out of print. She and Eugen went to Ragged Island in the summer—after a six-year hiatus—in hopes that being by the sea would raise their spirits and revive Vincent's health. It did; a friend who visited them on the island in September noted that Vincent was glowing, healthy, high-spirited, and bright-eyed. She swam naked in the waves and boiled lobsters for everyone.

But when she and Eugen returned to Steepletop, she disintegrated again. Her nerves were so raw that she couldn't even tolerate the sound of the telephone ringing, and she had Eugen rip it out. To add to her torment, Arthur Davison Ficke died on November 30. A month later, Vincent made out a one-page will in nearly illegible, down-sloping handwriting that illustrates the turbulence of her mental and emotional state. She left everything to Eugen, or, if he should no longer be living at the time of her death, to Norma.

Not until the spring of 1946 did she start to emerge from her long decline, eschewing drugs and alcohol at last. In August she responded to a letter Edmund Wilson had sent her in 1944, explaining what she had been through. "For five years I had been writing nothing but propaganda. And I can tell you from my own experience, that there is nothing on this earth which can so much get on the nerves of a good poet, as the writing of bad poetry. Anyway, finally, I cracked up under it. I was in the hospital a long time."

She was finally writing good poems again, and she included a few with the letter: "Ragged Island," "Tranquility at length when autumn comes," and "To a

Vincent's study at Steepletop was her sanctuary; no one was permitted to enter without her permission. *Edna St. Vincent Millay Papers, Manuscript Division, Library of Congress, Washington, DC*

Snake," all of which were published in magazines over the course of the following year, and eventually in the posthumous volume *Mine the Harvest*, which Norma edited after Vincent's death.

When she and Eugen went back to Ragged Island in the summer of 1947, she wrote proudly to her doctor, "I am strong and muscular and brown from months of swimming in the sea and working in the hot sun. . . . I am clean of drugs now, and clean of alcohol; eight months without a drink, six months without even a drop of wine."

They stayed at Ragged Island into the autumn, and when they returned once more to Steepletop Vincent seemed to be fully back in stride, returning long-overdue letters and continuing to write poetry. Although she complained of numerous ailments, her fervor was unabated.

In January 1948 she was elected to the Academy of American Poets' Board of Chancellors, a position in which she would help select poets to receive fellowships. Although she had been deeply pleased to learn of her election, after carefully reviewing the board's rules, she decided she could not, in good conscience, serve.

She wrote a lengthy letter to the chancellors, explaining her opposition to one of the bylaws that obliged poets who received fellowships to "sing for their supper," as she put it, reporting on their activities every three months.

She also didn't appreciate the frequent suggestions from her publisher to publish new collections combining her earlier work with new pieces. Harper & Brothers, to whom she remained in debt, was naturally looking for ways to find new readers for an author in whom they had invested so much money. Vincent would have none of it.

If the "nice people down there at Harper's would just for a little while stop nagging me, I might be able to get some work done," she wrote to her editor. While she sympathized with her publisher, she claimed that the constant requests destroyed her peace of mind.

One August day in 1949 Eugen, suddenly feeling poorly, went to the doctor. He was sent to Albany for

X-rays, which indicated cancer in his right lung. An operation at Deaconess Hospital in Boston was scheduled for Friday, August 26.

Vincent and Eugen drove to Boston, arriving in the midst of a heat wave. The surgeons successfully removed his right lung and put him in an oxygen tent to recover. He was doing so well that within days the tent was removed. Vincent stayed by his side, helping him breathe, giving him the devoted attention he had given her through all her illnesses.

On the third day, August 29, she left the hospital to rest at the hotel. While she was gone, Eugen suffered a cerebral hemorrhage and died. He was 69 years old.

Eugen had written to Norma, and to several friends, about his upcoming operation. But Norma had not yet received his letter when a phone call came from Boston. It was Vincent and she said only, "Oh, sister." When Norma repeated the greeting, Vincent could not reply. It took but a moment for Norma to realize what had happened.

Eugen's body was cremated and his ashes buried near Cora's grave in the mountain laurel grove at Steepletop. A friend drove Vincent home. Other friends arrived, and all who loved her, from near or far, were deeply concerned as to her well-being.

And rightly so—within a few weeks of Eugen's death an ambulance arrived to take her to Doctors Hospital. Once admitted, she complained only of exhaustion but was diagnosed with cirrhosis of the liver, nutritional

This is one of the last photos of Eugen and Vincent together, taken in 1948 on the grounds of their beloved Steepletop. *Edna St. Vincent Millay Papers, Archives and Special Collections, Vassar College Libraries*

deficiency, and acute neurasthenia (a medical condition associated with emotional disturbance). Various medications were prescribed, and nurses were instructed not to leave her alone.

When Vincent returned to Steepletop after a month's stay in the hospital, she promised her worried friends that she would not commit suicide. Hired man John Pinnie continued to arrive daily to do the chores; local postmistress, Mary Herron, took care of her correspondence and accounting. Pinnie asked another local woman, Lena Rausch, to clean several days a week, and her husband, Bill, did small odd jobs for Vincent.

Through the autumn and winter Vincent did her best to carry on. With her helpers, she fixed up Steepletop. She took vitamins and ate nutritious food in spite of having no appetite. She wrote Norma that she had devised a "scheme which really works . . . splitting myself into two personalities, one the patient, one the nurse." The nurse cooked nutritious, appetizing, and attractive meals and routinely administered medication, while the patient obediently swallowed everything offered. She was managing, she assured her sister. "To pretend that it is not agony, would be silly. But I can cope."

She spent the holidays alone, playing the piano, and trying to simply ignore the time of year. On New Year's Eve she telephoned Eugen's family in Holland.

The weather was especially bad that winter, and spring was at least six weeks late, hitting Vincent particularly cruelly when she saw her first dandelion. Remembering how excited Eugen always got at the sight of the first dandelion, she crumpled and wept.

That summer she threw herself into a commission from the *Saturday Evening Post* to write a Thanksgiving poem. She couldn't bring herself to return to Ragged Island but hoped she would be able to the following year.

In the autumn, the Thanksgiving poem completed, she worked on a friend's translations of her beloved Latin poet, Catullus. She started handling her own correspondence. Her habit was to work late into the night, often into the early morning hours.

Sometime during the day of October 19, John Pinnie came into the house with wood for the fireplace. He saw Vincent, wearing a silk dressing gown and slippers, lying lifeless on the landing at the bottom of the staircase in the front foyer. He went for the local doctor, who proclaimed her dead. The cause of the fall and of her death remains unknown.

Later a note to Lena Rausch was found on the kitchen table. It holds the only clues to Vincent's last moments. "Dear Lena: This iron is set too high. Don't put it on where it says 'Linen'—or it will scorch the linen. Try it on 'Rayon'—and then, perhaps on 'Woollen'. And be careful not to *burn your fingers* when you shift it from one heat to another. It is 5:30 and I have been working all night. I am going to bed. Good morning—E. St. V. M."

Norma held a small funeral service at Steepletop a few days later, which was attended by neighbors and a few friends. Vincent's poems were read aloud, and Beethoven's "Appassionata" sonata was played on the piano. Her body was cremated and her ashes buried with Eugen's, near Cora. She was 58 years old; her candle had finally burned out.

But, oh, how she had lived! Her life had been extraordinary. She had satisfied the hunger of her early years for passion and adventure. She had experienced love, desire, pain, and grief. She had embraced struggle and adversity, anger and sorrow. Small as she was, she had lived a big life, stirring everyone who encountered her. And she had expressed her life's exuberance and intensity in impassioned, intelligent, and well-wrought poems that continue to move and inspire readers decades after her death.

Thou famished grave, I will not fill thee yet,
Roar though thou dost, I am too happy here;
Gnaw thine own sides, fast on; I have no fear
Of thy dark project, but my heart is set
On living—I have heroes to beget
Before I die; I will not come anear
Thy dismal jaws for many a splendid year;
Till I be old, I aim not to be eat.
I cannot starve thee out: I am thy prey
And thou shalt have me; but I dare defend
That I can stave thee off; and I dare say,
What with the life I lead, the force I spend,
I'll be but bones and jewels on that day,
And leave thee hungry, even in the end.

—Sonnet, from Huntsman, What Quarry?, *1939*

Epilogue

After Vincent's death Norma and Charles moved into Steepletop, where they lived until Charles's death in 1976 and Norma's in 1986. Norma tended to her sister's legacy fiercely, preserving the many diaries, letters, photographs, and other family memorabilia that made it possible for this book, and others before it, to be written. (In 1998 some of the material was acquired by the Library of Congress.) She edited Vincent's final volume of poems, *Mine the Harvest*, which was published in 1954, and the *Collected Poems*, which came out in 1956, as well as helping to compile *Letters of Edna St. Vincent Millay*, which was published in 1952.

For the 36 years that she lived there after Vincent's death, Norma kept Steepletop exactly as it had been during Vincent's lifetime. In 1972 it was placed on the National Register of Historic Places. In 1973 Norma established the Millay Colony for the Arts, which still exists today. For more than 40 years, visual artists, writers, and composers have come to Steepletop for one-month residencies, during which they can devote themselves to their art.

The Edna St. Vincent Millay Society, dedicated to illuminating the poet's life and writings and preserving and interpreting the character of Steepletop, was founded in 1978. Today the Millay Society is in the process of restoring Steepletop and its grounds, including Vincent's extensive gardens. In June 2010 Steepletop was opened to the public, and every year another room or part of the grounds is ready for visitors, who come to pay tribute to the tiny, red-haired, high-spirited girl who became the most celebrated American poet of her time.

Steepletop
440 East Hill Road
Austerlitz, NY 12017
(518) 392-3362
www.millay.org

Acknowledgments

Publication of this book is truly a dream come true for me, many years in the making. I want to thank everyone who helped it come into being, beginning with Nancy Milford and Daniel Mark Epstein, authors of the 2001 adult biographies on Vincent, *Savage Beauty* and *What Lips My Lips Have Kissed*, respectively. I devoured both these books when they first appeared, and relied on them greatly in developing my own book proposal and for my initial research. And I am especially grateful to the late Norma Millay for preserving everything to do with the Millays.

Thanks to my agent, Jennifer Unter, for working so hard to inspire interest in this book, and to my editor Lisa Reardon, for her excitement, enthusiasm, and belief in it, as well as her intelligent guidance throughout the editing process. Thanks to Ellen Hornor and everybody at Chicago Review Press who contributed their expertise to make my book as good as it could possibly be.

I'm tremendously grateful to the wonderful artist Gabi Swiatkowska for so swiftly and beautifully illustrating young Vincent's portrait for the cover, and to her daughter Żak Kombel for her colorizing work.

Great thanks to Holly Peppe, Edna St. Vincent Millay's literary executor, for granting permission for me to quote so extensively from the Millays' writings and for so carefully reviewing the manuscript. Any errors that escaped her sharp eyes are mine. Thanks, too, to Fred Courtright of the Permissions Company for executing the permissions agreement, to Mark O'Berski of the Millay Society for providing the photo of Steepletop, and to Dawn Hagin of Lark Hotels for use of the Whitehall photo. For permission to quote from people important in Vincent's life, I thank Nancy Kuhl, curator of poetry, Yale Collection of American Literature at the Beinecke Rare Book and Manuscript Library, Yale University (Arthur Davison Ficke), and Stephen Schwartz, executive director, the Witter Bynner Foundation for Poetry (Hal Bynner), as well as publishers Henry Holt and Company (Floyd Dell's *Homecoming*) and Farrar, Straus and Giroux (Edmund Wilson's *The Shores of Light*).

Researching Vincent's life has been one of the most exciting endeavors of my life. I want to thank Dean Rogers, library specialist at Vassar College's Archives and Special Collections Library for his attentive help in my research, and the very efficient librarians in the Manuscript Division at the Library of Congress, one of this country's great treasures. I especially want to thank Margaret Kiechefer at the Library of Congress for her technical help in obtaining many of the photos used in this book.

In one of those unbelievable moments of serendipity, while completing my manuscript, I made a new friend—who turned out to be the granddaughter of writer Floyd Dell, a major figure in Vincent's life. Talking with Jerri Dell about her grandfather and Vincent has been a rich and delightful experience, and I'm thankful to her for sharing her grandfather's unpublished writings about Vincent with me.

Thank you to Ann Vartanian, friend and hostess extraordinaire, for receiving me so often in her beautiful home in Austerlitz, just across the road from Steepletop. Thank you to Emily Arnold McCully for her interest in my book and for her generous reading of my manuscript. Warmest thanks go to my dear friends Lucy Warner Kuemmerlee and Ann Scott Knight for insight and guidance as I shaped the early sections of the book.

I am deeply grateful to all those who share and enrich my life and work, most of all Anna Goddu and Jack Goddu, who never cease to inspire me, and Tom Farrell, whose love and care are boundless.

Time Line

February 22, 1892	Edna St. Vincent Millay is born in Rockland, Maine
December 28, 1893	Norma Lounella Millay is born
May 19, 1896	Kathleen Kalloch Millay is born
1900	Cora Millay asks Henry Millay to move out; Cora and the girls move to Rockport, Maine
1901	Cora and the girls move to Newburyport, Massachusetts
1904	Cora and the girls move to Camden, Maine
October 1906	Vincent's first poem is published in *St. Nicholas* magazine

March 1907	Vincent's poem "The Land of Romance" wins the *St. Nicholas* gold medal and garners critical attention from Edward Wheeler, editor of *Current Literature*
June 1909	Vincent graduates from high school
May 1912	Vincent submits "Renascence" to *The Lyric Year* competition
August 1912	Vincent recites "Renascence" at Whitehall, striking the attention of Caroline Dow, who raises funds for her to attend Vassar College
September 1913	Vincent begins studies at Vassar College
June 1917	Vincent graduates from Vassar College
September 1917	Vincent moves to New York City
December 1917	Vincent's first book of verse, *Renascence and Other Poems*, is published
Spring 1920	Vincent's second book, *A Few Figs from Thistles*, is published, establishing her reputation as the "It Girl" of Greenwich Village
December 1920	Kathleen Millay marries playwright Howard Young

January 1921	Vincent sails for Europe as foreign correspondent for *Vanity Fair* magazine
October 1921	Norma Millay marries painter Charles Ellis
August 1921	*Second April* is published
May 1923	Vincent wins the Pulitzer Prize for Poetry
July 18, 1923	Vincent marries Eugen Boissevain
November 1923	*The Harp-Weaver and Other Poems* is published
Spring 1925	Vincent and Eugen buy Steepletop in Austerlitz, New York
August 1927	Vincent marches in protest against Sacco and Vanzetti's executions
September 1928	*The Buck in the Snow* is published
February 5, 1931	Cora Millay dies at the age of 67
April 1931	*Fatal Interview* is published, becoming Vincent's first book to make the bestseller list
November 1934	*Wine from These Grapes* is published
December 1935	Henry Millay dies at the age of 71
July 1937	*Conversation at Midnight* is published

1938	A national poll declares Vincent one of the 10 most famous women in America
May 1939	*Huntsman, What Quarry?* is published
November 1940	*Make Bright the Arrows* is published; Vincent is elected to the American Academy of Arts and Letters
1942	Vincent writes "The Murder of Lidice" in response to Nazi razing of Lidice, Czechoslovakia
January 1943	Vincent receives Poetry Society of America's Frost Medal for distinguished lifetime achievement in poetry
September 1943	Kathleen Millay Young dies at the age of 47
August 29, 1949	Eugen Boissevain dies at the age of 69
October 19, 1950	Edna St. Vincent Millay dies at the age of 58
1954	*Mine the Harvest* is published posthumously
May 16, 1986	Norma Millay Ellis dies at the age of 92

Notes

Introduction

"I'll slap your face!": Millay to Arthur Davison Ficke, 15 December 1912, in *Letters of Edna St. Vincent Millay*, ed. Allan Ross Mac-dougall, 22.

1: A Girl Called Vincent

"There was a man who had two sons": Milford, *Savage Beauty: The Life of Edna St. Vincent Millay*, 50.

"I'd bend down": Milford, *Savage Beauty*, 9.

"It knocked the wind": Milford, *Savage Beauty*, 24.

"One bird on a tree": "Poetical Works of Vincent Millay," 1908, Edna St. Vincent Millay Papers, Manuscript Division, Library of Congress, Washington, DC.

"All my childhood": Millay to Tess Root, 24 August 1923, in *Letters*, 176.

"Your papa ought": Henry Millay to Millay, 25 May 1900, ESVM Papers (LOC).

"Tell Mama . . . Papa is earning": Henry Millay to Millay, 2 July 1900, ESVM Papers (LOC).

"It seems an awful long time": Henry Millay to Millay, 20 November 1900, ESVM Papers (LOC).

2: Four Homes in Two Years

"Dear Mama: I thought": Millay to Cora Millay, 7 November 1900, ESVM Papers (LOC).

"You said you were": Milford, *Savage Beauty*, 30.

"More than ordinary cleanliness": Johnson & Johnson, "Typhoid Fever" Contagious Disease Bulletin No. 29, 1901.

"a weekly journal": Peter Hutchinson, "A Publisher's History of American Magazines: Major Publishers Enter the Magazine Market," 2011, http://themagazinist.com/uploads/Harpers_Young_People.pdf.

"Salisbury, Mass.": Millay to Harper & Brothers, 12 February 1902, in *Letters*, 5.

"And many a night": Epstein, *What Lips My Lips Have Kissed: The Loves and Love Poems of Edna St. Vincent Millay*, 6.

3: A Very Young Housekeeper

"Excuse me, Miss Harrington": Milford, *Savage Beauty*, 5.

"I'm the Queen of the Dish-pan": "Poetical Works of Vincent Millay," 1908, ESVM Papers (LOC).

"a scrawny girl": Epstein, *What Lips*, 15.

"the poem . . . seems to us": Edward Wheeler, "The Land of Romance," *Current Literature*, vol. 42, no. 4, April 1907, 456–57.

"I am going to play Susie": Edna St. Vincent Millay diary entry, 25 March 1907, ESVM Papers (LOC).

"How I hate to have her go!": Edna St. Vincent Millay diary entry, 20 March 1907, ESVM Papers (LOC).

"My part is going to be great": Edna St. Vincent Millay diary entry, 25 March 1907, ESVM Papers (LOC).

"*Triss* went off": Edna St. Vincent Millay diary entry, 8 April 1907, ESVM Papers (LOC).

4: A Person of Intense Moods

"Dearest, when you go away": "Poetical Works of Vincent Millay,"
1908, ESVM Papers (LOC).

"To My Mother": "Poetical Works of Vincent Millay," 1908, ESVM
Papers (LOC).

"lots of spark and spunk": Milford, *Savage Beauty*, 34.

"the life of the party": Epstein, *What Lips*, 21.

"Vincent made everything": Epstein, *What Lips*, 21.

"the spirit of the house": "The Millays as I Knew Them," *The Columns*, April 1938, ESVM Papers (LOC).

"My God is all gods": Edna St. Vincent Millay diary entry, 28 June
1908, ESVM Papers (LOC).

"I guess I'm going to explode": Edna St. Vincent Millay diary entry,
29 June 1908, ESVM Papers (LOC).

"Such a lovely day": Edna St. Vincent Millay diary entry, 30 June
1908, ESVM Papers (LOC).

"I've written so many verses": Edna St. Vincent Millay diary entry,
19 July 1908, ESVM Papers (LOC).

"I think I'll call her": Edna St. Vincent Millay diary entry, 19 July
1908, ESVM Papers (LOC).

"Now, Muvver": "The Dear Incorrigibles," 1908, ESVM Papers
(LOC).

"There is a boy": Edna St. Vincent Millay diary entry, 17 April
1909, ESVM Papers (LOC).

"The world and I": "Poetical Works of Vincent Millay," 1908,
ESVM Papers (LOC).

5: Good-bye to Girlhood

"I'm here!": Millay to Norma Millay, 16 July 1909, ESVM Papers
(LOC).

"and we payed": Norma Millay to Millay, 4 August 1909, ESVM
Papers (LOC).

"two or three free rides": Kathleen Millay to Millay, 23 July 1909,
ESVM Papers (LOC).

"Of course I had": Edna St. Vincent Millay diary entry, 30 September 1909, ESVM Papers (LOC).

"One hooked me up": Epstein, *What Lips*, 20–21.

"I have only a few minutes": Millay to Cora Millay, [n.d.] December, ESVM Papers (LOC).

"I've sat here all the afternoon": *St. Nicholas*, May 1910, Edna St. Vincent Millay Papers, Archives and Special Collections, Vassar College Libraries.

"Words cannot express": Edna St. Vincent Millay diary entry, 16 April 1910, ESVM Papers (LOC).

"disgracefully short": Edna St. Vincent Millay diary entry, 16 March 1910, ESVM Papers (LOC).

"Bach and I are getting acquainted": Edna St. Vincent Millay diary entry, 6 January 1910, ESVM Papers (LOC).

"Read some of the Sonnets": Edna St. Vincent Millay diary entry, 15 March 1910, ESVM Papers (LOC).

"Of course I'm not": Edna St. Vincent Millay diary entry, 26 April 1910, ESVM Papers (LOC).

"The devil is in the polka-dots": Edna St. Vincent Millay diary entry, 23 April 1910, ESVM Papers (LOC).

"pupils as old": Edna St. Vincent Millay diary entry, 18 May 1910, ESVM Papers (LOC).

"Shall I not know": Edna St. Vincent Millay "Journal of a Little Girl Grown-Up" entry, July 1910, ESVM Papers (LOC).

"Am awfully homesick": Millay to Cora Millay, 29 July 1910, ESVM Papers (LOC).

"I met my fate": Edna St. Vincent Millay diary entry, 31 October 1910, ESVM Papers (LOC).

"the dearest little witch costume": Edna St. Vincent Millay diary entry, 31 October 1910, ESVM Papers (LOC).

"I've tried to keep": Edna St. Vincent Millay diary entry, 3 January 1911, ESVM Papers (LOC).

"To you who, though yet but a shadow": Edna St. Vincent Millay diary entry, 3 April 1911, ESVM Papers (LOC).

"I have come to say goodbye": Edna St. Vincent Millay diary entry, 27 June 1910, ESVM Papers (LOC).

"My life is but a seeking": Edna St. Vincent Millay "Vincent Millay—Her Book" entry, 3 July 1910, ESVM Papers (LOC).
"I'm getting old and ugly": Edna St. Vincent Millay "Vincent Millay—Her Book" entry, 10 October 1910, ESVM Papers (LOC).

6: The Poem That Raised a Furor

"with everything,—myself": Edna St. Vincent Millay "Vincent Mil-
lay—Her Book" entry, 3 January 1912, ESVM Papers (LOC).
"I do not think": Edna St. Vincent Millay "Vincent Millay—Her
Book" entry, 11 February 1912, ESVM Papers (LOC).
"Good morning!": Edna St. Vincent Millay "Vincent Millay—Her
Book" entry, 22 February 1912, ESVM Papers (LOC).
"Mr. Millay is very ill": Edna St. Vincent Millay "Sweet and
Twenty" entry, 19 September 1912, ESVM Papers (LOC).
"I was not the least bit": Edna St. Vincent Millay "Sweet and
Twenty" entry, 19 September 1912, ESVM Papers (LOC).
"found Papa very low": Edna St. Vincent Millay "Vincent Millay—
Her Book" entry, 2 March 1912, ESVM Papers (LOC).
"He's had pneumonia": Millay to Cora Millay, 4 March 1912,
ESVM Papers (LOC).
"Papa is better": Millay to Cora Millay, 4 March 1912, ESVM
Papers (LOC).
"a voice with a future": Millay to Cora, Norma, and Kathleen Mil-
lay, 17 March 1912, ESVM Papers (LOC).
"I pop in and out": Millay to Cora, Norma, and Kathleen Millay, 17
March 1912, ESVM Papers (LOC).
"down under ground": Epstein, *What Lips*, 53.
"You have been": Norma Millay to Millay, 20 March 1912, ESVM
Papers (LOC).
"Ella thinks she's going to die": Millay to Cora, Norma, and Kath-
leen Millay, 17 March 1912, ESVM Papers (LOC).
"This seems to be": Cora Millay to Millay, 21 March 1912, ESVM
Papers (LOC).
"It may astonish you": Millay to Ferdinand Earle, July [n.d.], ESVM
Papers (LOC).

"Dear and true Poetess!": Ferdinand Earle to Millay, 6 August 1912, ESVM Papers (LOC).

"This, then, is what I have been": Millay to Ferdinand Earle, 5 November 1912, ESVM Papers (LOC).

"I realized it was an unmerited": Orrick Johns, *Letters*, 18.

"the best thing in the book": Edna St. Vincent Millay "Sweet and Twenty" entry, 14 November 1912, ESVM Papers (LOC).

"the young girl": Epstein, *What Lips*, 67.

"she should be admitted": Virginia Gildersleeve to Talcott Williams, 18 January 1913, ESVM Papers (Vassar).

"Let us by all means": Virginia Gildersleeve to Talcott Williams, 27 January 1913, ESVM Papers (Vassar).

"Some people think": Edna St. Vincent Millay "Vincent Millay—Her Book" entry, 10 January 1913, ESVM Papers (LOC).

"drop of red, red blood": Edna St. Vincent Millay "Vincent Millay—Her Book" entry, 10 January 1913, ESVM Papers (LOC).

7: Hello, New York!

"Fancy! After all these years": Edna St. Vincent Millay "Sweet and Twenty" entry, 7 February 1913, ESVM Papers (LOC).

"The hot water": Millay to Ella McCaleb, 12 July 1913, ESVM Papers (Vassar).

"buildings everywhere": Millay to Cora, Norma, and Kathleen Millay, 5 February 1913, ESVM Papers (LOC).

"a pair of black satin pumps": Millay to Cora, Norma, and Kathleen Millay, February 1913, ESVM Papers (LOC).

"a brawny male of forty-five": Arthur Davison Ficke to Ferdinand Earle, 3 December 1912, in *Letters*, 18. Cited with permission of Yale University.

"I am going crazy": Edna St. Vincent Millay "Sweet and Twenty" entry, 27 April 1913, ESVM Papers (LOC).

"He has invited": Edna St. Vincent Millay "Sweet and Twenty" entry, April 1913, ESVM Papers (LOC).

"Miss Millay has perhaps": Ella McCaleb to Caroline Dow, 23 June 1913, ESVM Papers (Vassar).

"Yes, indeed, I'm coming!": Millay to Ella McCaleb, 7 July 1913, ESVM Papers (Vassar).

"I wonder if I ought": Millay to Ella McCaleb, 7 July 1913, ESVM Papers (Vassar).

8: The Pink-and-Gray College

"I was prepared": Edna St. Vincent Millay, History Entrance Exam, September 1913, ESVM Papers (Vassar).

"an excellent student": Florence G. Jenney, *Russell Sage Alumnae Quarterly*, Winter 1951, ESVM Papers (Vassar).

"She could not": Florence G. Jenney, *Russell Sage Alumnae Quarterly*, Winter 1951, ESVM Papers (Vassar).

"I hate this pink-and-gray college": Millay to Arthur Davison Ficke, 1913–14 [n.d.], in *Letters*, 48.

"getting so crazy": Milford, *Savage Beauty*, 114.

"she was one of the celebrities": Milford, *Savage Beauty*, 108.

"handsome quiet big child": Edna St. Vincent Millay, "Sweet and Twenty" entry, 5 December 1913, ESVM Papers (LOC).

"I have paid $10.50": Milford, *Savage Beauty*, 115.

"slight and dainty": *Poughkeepsie Eagle*, 12 October 1915, ESVM Papers (Vassar).

"hockey hero, cheer-leader": Millay to Norma Millay, 14 November 1914, ESVM Papers (LOC).

"your hair all *simple*": Millay to Cora, Norma, and Kathleen Millay, June 1915, ESVM Papers (LOC).

"Dearest little old sweetheart": Elaine Ralli to Millay, postmarked 18 December 1915, ESVM Papers (LOC).

"frankness, intensity and dramatic feeling": Epstein, *What Lips*, 147.

"We drove around": Charlotte Babcock, "Letter to the Editor," *Vassar Alumnae Quarterly*, 1960, ESVM Papers (Vassar).

"all the way through college": Ella MacCaleb to Cora Millay, 13 June 1917, ESVM Papers (LOC).

9: The "It Girl" of Greenwich Village

"oh, *wonderful!*": Millay to Millay family, 3 September 1917, ESVM Papers (LOC).

"dressed me up": Millay to Cora and Norma Millay, 22 September 1916, ESVM Papers (LOC).

"It is eleven o'clock": Millay to Cora and Norma Millay, 27 October 1917, ESVM Papers (LOC).

"I'm as crazy": Millay to Norma Millay, 24 November 1917, in *Letters*, 83.

"A slender little girl": Dell, *Homecoming: An Autobiography*, 301. Copyright © 1933, 1961 by Floyd Dell. Reprinted by permission of Henry Holt and Company, LLC.

"Never ask a girl poet": Floyd Dell, "Not Roses, Roses All the Way: Recollections of Edna St. Vincent Millay," Unpublished essay (1961). Reprinted by permission of Jerri Dell.

"I had not known": Edward J. Wheeler to Millay, 12 December 1917, ESVM Papers (LOC).

"Oh girls, your mother": Cora Millay to Millay and Norma Millay, 9 January 1918, ESVM Papers (LOC).

"like a wonderful brother": Norma Millay to Cora Millay, 24 January 1918, ESVM Papers (LOC).

"he's exceedingly handsome": Epstein, *What Lips*, 133.

"Mrs. Millay cut her hair": Dell, *Homecoming*, 307.

"most extraordinary": Wilson, *The Shores of Light: A Literary Chronicle of the 1920s and 1930s*, 760. Copyright © 1952 by Edmund Wilson. Copyright renewed © 1980 by Helen Miranda Wilson. Reprinted by permission of Farrar, Straus and Giroux, LLC.

"rotten work": Kathleen Millay to Millay family, 10 November 1918, ESVM Papers (LOC).

"the light from": Walter Adolphe Roberts, "Tiger Lily," Unpublished memoir, ESVM Papers (Vassar).

"the most beautiful": Jeff Kennedy, "A History of the Provincetown Playhouse," 2014, http://www.provincetownplayhouse.com/history.html.

"I have never made": Millay to the Millay family, 26 February 1920, ESVM Papers (LOC).

"the company hushed": Wilson, *Shores of Light*, 750.

"that it was difficult": Wilson, *Shores of Light*, 755.

"I am becoming very famous": Millay to Harold Witter Bynner, 29 October 1920, in *Letters*, 102.

10: European Adventures

"I was awake": Millay to Cora Millay, 13 January 1921, ESVM Papers (LOC).

"miles and miles": Millay to Norma Millay, 20 January 1921, ESVM Papers (LOC).

"I have been really homesick": Millay to Cora Millay, 18 January 1921, ESVM Papers (LOC).

"Dearest Darling Baby Sister": Millay to Norma Millay, 25 May 1921, ESVM Papers (LOC).

"the seashore": Millay to Cora Millay, 23 July 1921, ESVM Papers (LOC).

"possibly in a newer form": Millay to Cora Millay, September [n.d.], ESVM Papers (LOC).

"She never clutters": Frances Lester Warner, Review of Edna St. Vincent Millay's *Second April*, *Atlantic Monthly: A Magazine of Literature, Science, Art, and Politics*, vol. 128 (October 1921), 432.

"in spite of all the hardships": Millay to Cora Millay, 15 November 1921, ESVM Papers (LOC).

"If you should ever": Norma Millay to Millay, 23 October 1921, ESVM Papers (LOC).

"For many years": Arthur Davison Ficke to Millay, 22 November 1921, ESVM Papers (LOC). Cited with permission of Yale University.

"bound in the memories": Millay to Harold Witter Bynner, 23 December 1921, in *Letters*, 139.

"Do you really want me": Millay to Harold Witter Bynner, 23 December 1921, in *Letters*, 139.

"YES HAL": Milford, *Savage Beauty*, 224.

"is something to me": Millay to Harold Witter Bynner, 23 January 1922, ESVM Papers (LOC).

"PREPARE SAIL": Millay to Cora Millay, 2 March 1922, ESVM Papers (LOC).

"fried sauerkraut": Millay to Norma Millay, 11 May 1922, ESVM Papers (LOC).

"working itself out beautifully": Millay to Horace Liveright, November 1922, in *Letters*, 167.

"I have been quite respectably": Millay to Isobel Simpson, 15 December 1922, in *Letters*, 168.

"marvelous . . . I shall love you": Millay to Arthur Davison Ficke, 17 December 1922, in *Letters*, 168.

11: An Embarrassment of Riches

"They acted their parts": Dell, *Homecoming*, 308.

"Darling, do you remember": Millay to Cora Millay, 30 May 1923, ESVM Papers (LOC).

"Inez Milholland": Millay to Norma Millay, 3 March 1914, ESVM Papers (LOC).

"You go ahead": Epstein, *What Lips*, 170.

"tied down by membranes": Epstein, *What Lips*, 177.

Miss Millay Under Knife and other headlines: 19 July 1923, ESVM Papers (LOC).

"sleeps like a guinea pig": Epstein, *What Lips*, 179.

"Of course, it has made": Millay to Cora Millay, 7 November 1923, ESVM Papers (LOC).

"poet-girl": *Rochester Democrat and Chronicle*, February 14, 1924.

"wistful, appealing": *Rochester Democrat and Chronicle*, February 15, 1924.

"It is considered": Millay to Norma Millay, 4 May 1924, ESVM Papers (LOC).

"strong and husky": Eugen Boissevain to Cora Millay, 18 August 1924, ESVM Papers (LOC).

"one of the loveliest places": Millay to Cora Millay, 22 June 1925, in *Letters*, 194.

"dulled by routine acts": Allan Ross Macdougall, "Husband of a Genius," *Delineator*, October 1934.

"by turn gay and grave": "Edna St. Vincent Millay Reads Her Poems at Literary Institute," *Christian Science Monitor*, May 6, 1925.

"Solely for use": Millay to Bert and Rose Millay, 15 October 1926, in *Letters*, 211.

12: The Poet as Celebrity

"The greatest American opera!": *New Yorker*, February 26, 1927, 61.

"That the amount of royalties": Edna St. Vincent Millay diary entry, 9 March 1927, ESVM Papers (LOC).

"The Three Graces": Edna St. Vincent Millay diary entry, 29 April 1927, ESVM Papers (LOC).

"very courteous . . . but gave me": Edna St. Vincent Millay diary entry, 22 August 1927, ESVM Papers (LOC).

"Does no faint shadow": Millay to Governor Alvan T. Fuller, 22 August 1927, in *Letters*, 222.

"So I knew": Edna St. Vincent Millay diary entry, 23 August 1927, ESVM Papers (LOC).

"devoted . . . an enchanted sickness": Milford, *Savage Beauty*, 306.

"But there's nothing": Millay to Llewelyn Powys, 20 April 1932, in *Letters*, 244.

"gives evidence": Louise Bogan, *Poetry: A Magazine of Verse*, February 1935, 277–79.

"the only thing": Millay to Professor Herbert C. Lipscomb, 6 October 1936, in *Letters*, 284.

"On an occasion, then": Millay to the secretary of New York University, 22 May 1937, in *Letters*, 291.

America's Foremost Woman Poet: *McCall's*, July 1937.

"If you don't change": Charles Norman, Associated Press, 1937, ESVM Papers (Vassar).

13: The Flickering Candle

"vehement, mettlesome": *Worcester Telegram*, January 12, 1939.

"more susceptible to pain": Connie M. Guion to Eugen Boissevain, 21 November 1939, ESVM Papers (LOC).

"there are a few good poems": Millay to George Dillon, 29 November 1940, in *Letters*, 309.

"hastily written and hotheaded pieces": Millay to Cass Canfield, 8 January 1946, in *Letters*, 329.

"Miss Millay may have written": Peter Monro Jack, *New York Times Book Review*, December 1, 1940.

"what I am trying to do": Millay to Charlotte Babcock Sills, 2 January 1941, in *Letters*, 310–12.

"For five years": Millay to Edmund Wilson, August 1946, in *Letters*, 333.

"I am strong": Millay to Foster Kennedy, 7 March 1947, ESVM Papers (LOC).

"sing for their supper": Millay to the Chancellors of the Academy of American Poets, 2 February 1948, in *Letters*, 345–46.

"nice people down there at Harper's": Millay to Cass Canfield, 10 May 1948, in *Letters*, 347.

"Oh, sister": Milford, *Savage Beauty*, 497–98.

"scheme which really works": Millay to Norma Millay, 27 January 1950, in *Letters*, 363–64.

"Dear Lena": Millay to Lena Rausch, [n.d.] 1950, in *Letters*, 376.

Bibliography

Books About Edna St. Vincent Millay

Cheney, Anne. *Millay in Greenwich Village*. Tuscaloosa: University of Alabama Press, 1975.

Dell, Floyd. *Homecoming: An Autobiography*. Port Washington, NY: Kennikat Books, 1969. Reprint of original edition published by Farrar & Rinehart in 1933.

Epstein, Daniel Mark. *What Lips My Lips Have Kissed: The Loves and Love Poems of Edna St. Vincent Millay*. New York: Henry Holt, 2001.

Gould, Jean. *The Poet and Her Book: A Biography of Edna St. Vincent Millay*. New York: Dodd, Mead, 1969.

Gurko, Miriam. *Restless Spirit: The Life of Edna St. Vincent Millay*. New York: Thomas Y. Crowell Company, 1962.

Milford, Nancy. *Savage Beauty: The Life of Edna St. Vincent Millay*. New York: Random House, 2001.

Millay, Edna St. Vincent. *Letters of Edna St. Vincent Millay*. Edited by Allan Ross Macdougall. New York: Harper & Brothers, 1952.

Shafter, Toby. *Edna St. Vincent Millay: America's Best-Loved Poet*. New York: Julian Messner, 1957.

Sheean, Vincent. *The Indigo Bunting: A Memoir of Edna St. Vincent Millay*. New York: Shocken Books, 1973. Reprint of original edition published by Harper & Row in 1951.

Wilson, Edmund. *The Shores of Light: A Literary Chronicle of the 1920s and 1930s*. Boston: Northeastern University Press, 1985. Reprint of original edition published by Farrar, Straus and Young in 1952.

Books by Edna St. Vincent Millay

Poetry

Renascence and Other Poems. New York: Mitchell Kennerley, 1917.

A Few Figs from Thistles: Poems and Four Sonnets, Salvo One. New York: Frank Shay, 1920.

Second April. New York: Mitchell Kennerley, 1921.

The Ballad of the Harp-Weaver. New York: Frank Shay, 1922.

The Harp-Weaver and Other Poems. New York: Harper & Brothers, 1923.

The Buck in the Snow. New York: Harper & Brothers, 1928.

Edna St. Vincent Millay's Poems Selected for Young People. New York: Harper & Brothers, 1929.

Fatal Interview. New York: Harper & Brothers, 1931.

Wine from These Grapes. New York: Harper & Brothers, 1934.

Baudelaire, Charles. *Les Fleurs du Mal*. Translated by George Dillon and Edna St. Vincent Millay as *The Flowers of Evil* (New York: Harper & Brothers, 1936).

Conversation at Midnight. New York: Harper & Brothers, 1937.

Huntsman, What Quarry? New York: Harper & Brothers, 1939.

Collected Lyrics. New York: Harper & Brothers, 1939.

Make Bright the Arrows: 1940 Notebook. New York: Harper & Brothers, 1940.

Collected Sonnets of Edna St. Vincent Millay. New York: Harper & Brothers, 1941.

The Murder of Lidice. New York: Harper & Brothers, 1942.

Mine the Harvest. Edited by Norma Millay. New York: Harper & Brothers, 1954.

Collected Poems. Edited by Norma Millay. New York: Harper & Brothers, 1956.

Edna St. Vincent Millay: Selected Poems—The Centenary Edition. Edited by Colin Falck. New York: HarperCollins, 1991.

Early Poems. Edited by Holly Peppe. New York: Penguin, 1998.

Poetry for Young People: Edna St. Vincent Millay. Edited by Frances Schoonmaker. New York: Sterling, 1999.

The Selected Poetry of Edna St. Vincent Millay. Edited by Nancy Milford. New York: Modern Library Classics, 2002.

Edna St. Vincent Millay: Selected Poems. Edited by J. D. McClatchy. New York: Library of America, 2003.

Collected Poems. Reissue of the 1956 edition, with new material by Holly Peppe. New York: Harper Perennial, 2001.

Plays

Aria da Capo. New York: Mitchell Kennerley, 1921.

The Lamp and the Bell. New York: Frank Shay, 1921.

Two Slatterns and a King: A Moral Interlude. Cincinnati: Stewart Kidd, 1921.

The King's Henchman. New York: Harper & Brothers, 1927.

The Princess Marries the Page. New York: Harper & Brothers, 1932.

Prose

Distressing Dialogues. [Nancy Boyd, pseud.] New York: Harper & Brothers, 1924.

Index